HAVE A GREAT DREAM
Book 1; The Overview

Decoding Your Dreams To
Discover Your Full Potential

By
Layne Dalfen

Copyright © 2018 Layne Dalfen

The Dream Interpretation Center (DICI) Inc.
3555 Cote des Neiges, Suite 2014
Montreal, Quebec, Canada, H3H 1V2
http://www.haveagreatdream.com

Dalfen, Layne , 1952 –
Have A Great Dream
Book 1; The Overview
Decoding Your Dreams To Discover Your Full Potential
Layne Dalfen

Deborah Joy Cafiero, Editor
Dawn James (Publish and Promote), Book Production
John Nyberg, Cover Photograph
Lisa Karachinsky, Cover Design, Dream Maps

Printed and bound in Canada
ISBN 978-0-9737205-3-2 (Paperback)
ISBN 978-0-9737205-1-8 (eBook)

Note to the reader: This book is not intended to dispense psychological or therapeutic advice. The information is provided for educational and inspirational purposes only. In the event, you use any of the information in this book for yourself, which is your constitutional right, the author and publisher assumes no responsibility for your actions. In some chapters, names and locations have been changed to protect privacy.

TABLE OF CONTENTS

ACKNOWLEDGMENTS

Thank you Andy, Lisa, Chelsea and Joshua, Emma-Jo, Marlee, Sophie and my late Mom too for believing in me. Your consistent support is forever in my heart.

Thank you Lisa, my creative daughter, for your beautiful book cover, and for your wonderful dream maps!! Thank you Craig Steinberg from WebByCraig.com for your input and for all you do in hosting and promoting my site, www.haveagreatdream.com

Thank you to Deborah Joy Cafiero. It is 18 years ago that we worked together on my book titled *Dreams Do Come True; Decoding Your Dreams To Discover Your Full Potential.* Back then I wrote in my acknowledgements about you, the following: "….my editor extraordinaire; whose patience, hard work, humor, persistence, opinionated opinions, honesty, brutality, and intelligence many times inspired me. Deborah Joy. I can say with confidence, after almost twenty years, you are not as brutal, but your opinionated opinions, honesty, humor, and hard work are still the driving force in my wonderful experience of working with you!

A note to readers: Please feel free to contact me. My web site address is http://www. haveagreatdream.com. You can reach me by email as well at info@haveagreatdream.com

Credits for pictures in Book 1; The Overview
1. The Dog Psychiatrist on Page 54. http://www.cartoonstock.com [6]
2. The Tree of Life on Page 65. Photo by veeterzy on Unsplash.com [5]
3. The Girl in the Bathtub on Page 89. http://www.twenty20.com [1]
4. Sisyphus on Page 96. http://www.istockphoto.com [2]
5. The Giraffe on Page 101. http://www.pixabay.com [3]
6. The Tug of War on Page 114. http://www.pixabay.com [3]
7. Niagara Falls on Page 124. © Lequint | http://www.dreamstime.com [4]

INTRODUCTION

My book titled *Dreams Do Come True: Decoding Your Dreams To Discover Your Full Potential* was first published in 2002. The second edition was recently released with the title, *Have A Great Dream, Book 2; A Deeper Discussion: Decoding Your Dreams To Discover Your Full Potential*.

My URL www.haveagreatdream.com uses the same name. I wrote this book, *Have A Great Dream, Book 1; The Overview* to focus closer on the first level of meaning in the dream. I am a first-things-first kind of woman. Since I wrote my first book, I've noticed how some clients want to go deep from the get-go, leaving me to respond, "Before we go deep, let's first find out what current situation in your life triggered this dream." If you just want to know why you had that dream last night, this book is for you! For those of you though, who *do* want to understand deeper meaning and the incredible gold to be found in investigating all that even one dream has to give you, you will find it all in *Have A Great Dream, Book 2; A Deeper Discussion.*

In the first half of this book I discuss various theories and methods you can employ to interpret your dreams and in doing so, will show you how to access the tools you need to change your life. In the second part, you will find detailed examples of dreams to practice with, and the theories I discussed in the first half will suddenly become very clear for you. I have tremendous faith in the power of dreamwork, for I have seen its positive effects on my own life and the lives of others.

After a crisis in my early twenties and eight years of Freudian psychoanalysis, I learned how to use my dreams to improve my life. More importantly, this experience motivated me to study the techniques for interpreting dreams according to different schools of psychology. At thirty, I earned my Certificate in Gestalt Counseling. Through my studies at the Center, I learned to interpret dreams from a Gestalt perspective. I wanted to explore beyond Freudian and Gestalt interpretation, so I took courses at The Alfred Adler Institute under the American Dr. Leo Gold. I later became a member of The C. G. Jung Society of

Montreal and the International Association for The Study of Dreams (IASD), where I was a Board Member from 2005 through to 2009.

I have found over the years that there is no single, "right" approach to understanding dreams. Each different school of dream theory has had something new to teach me, some new opportunity for me to change and grow through dreamwork. When I created The Dream Interpretation Center in 1997, I felt it was important to teach other people how to use different approaches to dream analysis. I encourage my clients to try out many avenues, because this leads to greater flexibility in behavior, increased self-awareness, and, ultimately, enhanced fulfillment and life satisfaction.

Dreams are a visual of our problem-solving skills turned to a current issue that is on our mind when we go to sleep at night. Where the conscious mind is adept at avoiding, the unconscious mind is ready to face it all. Further, our unconscious works night after night suggesting behaviors, pointing to strengths we need to tap into, and sometimes coming to direct conclusions about what needs to be done to solve the problem. Dreams provide us with a safe place to practice new behaviors. Eventually we can bring the new behavior out of the dream scenes and into waking life.

You are in the powerful position to choose how to respond to every situation in your life. Dream decoding is a great way to go beyond your habitual reactions to issues that come up in your life, and learn to replace them with new behaviors.

No one ever said that change is easy, but I am here to tell you, it most certainly is possible. The behaviors you wish you possessed are understood and acquired faster when you decode your dreams. You propel your problem-solving skills. Dream analysis allows you to become more imaginative and flexible in your responses to the plethora of predicaments that life throws at you.

Theories of Dream Interpretation

This workbook will help you transition to the practical tasks of interpreting your own dreams, but first you need some background on the different theories of dream interpretation. To that end I'm going to give a quick overview of the major thinkers in the field. This certainly isn't a complete description of thinkers like Freud or Jung, but a general idea of their dream interpretation theories will help you understand how the different techniques can clue you into your dream's meaning.

Sigmund Freud

Sigmund Freud, an Austrian neurologist from the late 19th to early 20th centuries, completely reimagined the field of psychology and many of his theories are still influential today. Freud was concerned with the hidden relationship between our conscious thoughts and actions and our unconscious mind. To uncover this relationship he invented a process called "free association." He considered this his greatest contribution to science. I agree.

Here is how Freud himself described free association. "...The patient should take up a restful position and close his eyes; he must be explicitly instructed to renounce all criticism of thought-formations which he may perceive. He must also be told that the success of the psychoanalysis depends upon his noting and communicating everything that passes through his mind, and that he must not allow himself to suppress one idea because it seems to him unimportant or irrelevant to the subject, or another because it seems nonsensical. He must preserve an absolute impartiality in respect to his ideas; for if he is unsuccessful in finding the desired solution of the dream, the obsessional idea, or the like, it will be because he permits himself to be critical of them" (Freud, 1938, p. 192).

Through free association and other techniques, Freud discovered that our thoughts, feelings and responses in the present reflect our relationships from the past, without our conscious awareness of this connection. It's like we have a filing cabinet tucked away in our unconscious mind, filled with our feelings and experiences from our lives. So when we experience something in our current life, our mind opens the filing cabinet and goes right to the section where we have had similar experiences in the past. The file from our memory plays back and gives us our initial reaction. I am calling it the initial reaction because hopefully, this book will help you decide if in fact you want your initial reaction to remain your only reaction.

Free association lets you open the filing cabinet consciously and actively. You can use your dreams to trigger the process of free association, for example by asking, "Does anyone in the dream spark a memory of someone I know?" Or you can try some of the following questions: "When have I felt this way before in my life?" or maybe, "Have I had this reaction somewhere else in my life?" or "Does this behavior feel familiar to me?" We'll see many examples of free association for dream interpretation in this workbook.

Because of his technique of free association, Freud became one of the first thinkers aware of the constant dance in our minds between the conscious and the unconscious, and between the past and present. Freud realized that dreams are always triggered by recent life experiences: "If I now consult my own experience with regard to the origin of the elements appearing in the dream-content, I must in the first place express the opinion that in every dream we may find some reference to the experiences of the preceding day. Whatever dream I turn to, whether my own or someone else's, this experience is always confirmed" (Freud, 1938, p. 239). Yet the dream is tied to our feelings and experiences from the past. Interpreting dreams through free association allows us to trace our current behaviors and feelings back to our past relationships, and to live with a greater awareness of our whole life's trajectory.

Carl Jung

Carl Gustave Jung was a Swiss psychiatrist and student of Freud. He learned from Freud that our conscious thoughts and behavior are the surface manifestation of our unconscious mind. Jung modified and extended some of Freud's theories of the mind, as well as his techniques for dream interpretation. For example, Jung modified the technique of free association to form a method called direct association, which is spontaneous but constantly comes back to the dream. Another idea of Jung's was to reenter the dream and change its imagery, using active imagination in order to develop the ideas put forth in the dream. We'll see examples of direct association and active imagination when we interpret particular dreams and the solutions they offer to the dreamer's life issues.

In analyzing his patients' dreams, Jung was looking for the whole picture. He wanted to understand how the dreamer was affected by and problem-solving her current issue. He would seek out the dreamer's reactions into the past for a clearer understanding of where she was coming from. But then Jung would take his understanding of the dream to a wider spectrum. He took it outward. Jung decided to look at those aspects of our dreams that seem similar to other people's dreams, or even to stories and images from around the world. Jung was the first thinker to really focus on how our dreams reflect our universal humanity and, in a sense, bring us all together.

He wanted us to take the dream, see it, and learn from it all that it could give us. That meant he didn't stop at the psychological learning, but instead continued into the spiritual realm. Carl Jung felt it was unavoidable to arrive at the spiritual aspects of dreams, because he knew that however we try to rationalize and deny the existence of fantasy, superstition, illusions, religion and mysticism in our psyche, we cannot escape this aspect of our "humanness." We are a combination of the rational and the mystical. That is what makes the whole of each of us. And our modern world has come to deny the very aspect we need to acknowledge and integrate.

I believe Jung wanted us to re-own the mystical, spiritual aspect of ourselves by seeking out the collective themes, stories, and characters in our dreams. Jung called this process of finding collective images amplification, because he thought of it as amplifying the details of your individual dream out to a universal framework. He believed these universal characters and images form the collective unconscious. Jung wrote, "I call it 'collective' because, unlike the personal unconscious, it is not made up of individual and more or less unique contents but of those which are universal and of regular occurrence" (Jung, 1989, p. 133). In this workbook, we will find that amplifying the themes of our dreams out to all humanity allows us to touch what is deepest and most spiritual in ourselves.

Perls: Gestalt Dream Interpretation

Dr. Jung said that each of us, newly born, starts out with a feeling of wholeness, a powerful and complete sense of the Self. This means we are born with all possibilities of behavior. We are giving; we are selfish. We are outgoing; we are shy. We are comfortable expressing our needs and we are not. We have the ability to feel frightened and we can be brave.

The people who bring us up send out messages. These messages might be direct or indirect, but somehow the messages ("You should do this," "You shouldn't do that!") reinforce that it is better to be one way than another. And so, through the years, we form "habits" for the behaviors we learn are acceptable. Then we forget about all the other ways of responding to events in our lives. You could say we become "overinvested" in a particular way of reacting. And of course, we become "underinvested" in the other parts of our psyche. It was Jung who first suggested that dreams can compensate for these distortions in the way we see things, slanted by the overinvested parts of our character (Jung, 1969. p. 62).

Fritz Perls adapted Jung's ideas by inventing a specific technique called Gestalt dream interpretation. In this technique the dreamer role-plays by speaking as the different parts of the dream in order to get in touch with his disowned parts. As Perls suggests, "You see how you can use everything in a dream. If you are pursued by an ogre in a dream, and you become the ogre, the nightmare disappears. You re-own the energy that is invested in the demon. Then the power of the ogre is no longer outside, alienated, but inside where you can use it" (Perls, 1992, p. 190). This works because all the parts of the dream are you. You are the producer, the director, and all the players. You are even the wall, the water, the road, the building, the snake, the monkey, and the monster. But the dreamer usually takes the role she most easily connects to in her waking life, and then gives out the other parts in the dream to people, animals, objects, things, and sometimes even places. The dreamer "projects" the alienated character traits that she needs onto something, someone, or some place else in the dream. So our dreams show us all the different parts we need to be fully ourselves, in every situation.

The most obvious advantage to speaking out as the different parts of the dream is that you are able to literally become that part of yourself. This can be extremely helpful when you need to access a certain character trait in your current situation, even though you have rejected it because of something that happened in your past. Perls describes what happens to us when we limit ourselves this way: "You do not allow yourself—or you are not allowed to be totally yourself. So your ego boundary shrinks more and more. Your power, your energy, becomes smaller and smaller. Your ability to cope with the world becomes less and less—and more and more rigid, more and more allowed only to cope as your character, as your preconceived pattern, prescribes it" (Perls, 1992, p. 31). If we always respond to events in the same way, we have little choice on how to proceed in a given situation. We need to access our "underinvested" or alienated parts. The disowned aspects of our character appear in our dreams when we need to use them. It is not by accident and it is not random.

Developing character traits as we need them in given situations is what Perls referred to as "maturation." It is what Jung called "individuation." They were saying the same thing. No matter whose writings I have read, everyone had his or her own way of expressing the importance of developing all our potential. Jung believed that the only sure way to maturation lies in our willingness to recognize and practice our disowned character traits. He called them our Shadows, because they are the opposite of the way we usually are. Without them we remain fragmented. With them we not only help ourselves respond to different situations, but we also become whole.

Alfred Adler: Take The Dream-Feeling and Run With It!

Like Jung, Adler was a student of Freud. Although Freud looked upon Adler as one of his first disciples, Adler never viewed himself that way and broke with Freud and Freudian psychoanalysis in 1911. Adler examined personality around the same time as Carl Jung and Sigmund Freud. They worked on some theories together until Adler rejected Freud's emphasis on sex, maintaining that personality difficulties are rooted in a feeling of inferiority deriving from restrictions on the individual's need for self-assertion.

Adler said our dreams give rise to emotions that help us move forward in waking life towards our goals. I call this theory, "Take that feeling and run with it." For example, the common dream of flying gives some of us such a glorious sense of freedom and fun! But I've seen flying dreams come to clients who feel down and depressed. Many people have so much pressure for a sustained period of time that they almost forget what it feels like to feel free; to feel good. For them a flying dream might be a reminder. It's a pick-me-up. Now that you have been reminded what that feels like, your solution is to take that feeling and find the time to give yourself a break in your waking life! Paint, run, exercise, play cards, see a movie, play a game, swim, ski, rest in the sun with a good book. Take the feeling the dream created and run with it!

After studying these four Fathers of Psychology I often find similar principles, viewed or named differently. They each had a slightly different slant to their theories. For example, Freud called Perl's "over-invested" character traits our habitual responses to life situations, sometimes known as repetition compulsion, in which we unconsciously attract certain people and situations to our life so that we can continue to play out our childhood behaviors and respond in the same way over and over. Adler called your over-invested parts, your Lifestyle.

Here's the thing I want to add about this concept, whether we call it our Lifestyle, over-invested parts, or habitual responses. All of them give us our sense of self. They give us our identity! And this identity also shapes how others expect us to respond in any given situation.

On an unconscious level we fear a loss of our identity if we were to respond differently than our "norm." This fear, while irrational, is somehow (for me anyway) easily understood. If you have been smoking for twenty-five years and your inner voice reprimands you daily, then by smoking you are perpetuating the reprimanding voice inside yourself that's been there since childhood. If you quit smoking, what will happen to the voice? Where and who will I be when I am not in a constant state of self-reproach?

Guy Corneau likened the act of trying a new response to laying the first brick of a new wall. The first day without a cigarette, you actually see for yourself you survived. You are still breathing. That's the first brick of your new identity as a non-smoker. The second successful day provides a second brick, and so on, until years later you see and more importantly "feel yourself" a non-smoker. You identify as a non-smoker.

By exploring various ways of describing our over-invested parts, we find different methods for expanding our responses. You know how Freud was always going back and looking into your past? Well, reaching back gives us the opportunity to understand more fully why we react the way we do. While Freud was looking back and Jung was looking out to the ideas, notions and experiences that all humans share, Adler was looking forward and using the feelings in the dream to move towards the solution to an issue we're experiencing. These are all paths towards creating a more flexible Lifestyle and a more fulfilling life.

CHAPTER ONE: WHY DID I HAVE THAT DREAM LAST NIGHT?

*T*he process of dream analysis is exactly the same as doing a puzzle. You try one piece. It doesn't fit, so you try another. I'm going to describe six basic approaches, which I call "points of entry" for solving your puzzle. If you are the dreamer you'll know when you have the right point of entry because it'll give you that "aha!" If you are working with the dreamer you'll know you've arrived by that wonderful expression seen on every dreamer's face when they catch their dream.

First of all, write the dream down. When you wake up with a dream in your mind, write down the dream story, double-spaced and with wide margins, on a sheet of paper—anything that gives you lots of room for jotting down notes and associations.

It's easiest to go through this the day you wake with the dream but even if you do it within a few days after, you'll catch the dream for sure! It's a dance. You are figuratively dancing inside the dream (looking at the events in the dream), and then coming outside the dream to events from your waking life, trying to uncover what situation the dream is mirroring. Dreaming is just another way of thinking. For me there is not much difference from the way we think at night or the way we think during the day. It's not as if you wake up in the morning and the curtain comes up and when you go to sleep the curtain goes down. One of the reasons I teach dream analysis is to help clients make what they are thinking in the day and thinking in the night more fluid. I do that because there is fluidity and I just want you to recognize it!

Decoding and Mapping the Dream

1. Isolate The Feelings.

After you've written a description of the dream, write down the feelings you had during the dream on the left side of the page, alongside the scenes where those feelings occurred. Pay particular attention to any changes in your feelings over the course of the dream, asking yourself how you felt at the beginning of the dream, as different characters appeared and events passed, and then at the end.

I have given you a dream map here that I divided into four sections, so you can see a map broken down step by step. You'll notice it's titled Danny's Giraffe Dream and later on in this workbook you will find the completed map along with the full analysis of Danny's dream.

How do you move from the dream-feelings into your waking life situation? Try asking yourself: What situation happened recently where you felt in a similar way to the way you felt in the dream? If your feelings changed over the course of the dream, is there an event that occurred recently in your life in which you started out feeling one way, and then progressed to another feeling?

Here's an example where the dream-feelings helped the dreamer identify her waking life problem to solve. In my first book, now titled *Have A Great Dream, Book 2; A Deeper Discussion: Decoding Your Dreams To Discover Your Full Potential*, I discuss a Picnic Dream in which the dreamer described how good she felt at the beginning of the dream being at a picnic, and then some ants crawling around started to make her feel uncomfortable. By the end of the dream she woke in a panic as the number of ants had grown considerably and were swarming the area. She was trying to push them away with her hands.

In this dream there was a progression of feelings that pointed to an escalating situation. When I asked the dreamer to consider whether she was experiencing a situation where she felt good at first but was lately feeling more and more uncomfortable, she clicked: a waking life situation with a lover had started out fun but was turning into an escalating problem that was starting to make her feel panicked.

Danny's Giraffe Dream

INTERESTED

I was watching a CNN news report alerting the public that a giraffe had escaped from the local zoo. The story featured a computer-generated giraffe moving rather than a film.

There was a map of Chicago in the background. Other people were in the room. I don't know who.

SHOCKED-
AMAZED
AWE +
PANIC

In the next scene I was at my mother's house. I got up and walked into the washroom. When I opened the door, to my amazement right there in the bathtub as big as life itself was the missing giraffe! I was shocked and in a complete panic.

CAUTIOUS

Not wanting to alarm the giraffe, I backed away slowly and closed the door. I immediately headed to the kitchen to call 911. I told them my name and gave my address, explaining I have the giraffe.

COMPLETE
SURPRISE
HOW SHE
APPEARS
FROM
NOWHERE
AS IF SHE
BELONGS

In the next scene, I was sitting at my mom's kitchen table with the anchor from CNN. She had piles of books around her and was looking up something in one book and then going to another. She's heavy set, wearing a track suit, and not very attractive looking.

Suddenly the bathroom door opened and my wife's cousin walked out, saying, "Hi you guys! How are you?"

Here's another example of a change in feelings. A woman dreamed she was playing with a puppy on the table. She thought the puppy was so cute and fun. Suddenly the dog made all over the table, and she found herself covered in you know what. This, as opposed to the Picnic Dream, was an instant rather than a gradual change.

When we considered whether the woman was experiencing a waking life situation with a sudden negative change in feelings, she found the mirror: she loved her job at first, but suddenly an abusive new boss was appointed who made her feel like you know what. The dream called her attention to take action and look for another place of employment.

If the "feelings" point of entry doesn't work, try the next one! Remember, it is just like doing a puzzle. Try another piece.

2. Identify The Symbols, Metaphors, or Characters.

Now isolate and circle each symbol that appears in your dream description. Basically, anything in a dream can be a symbol, including objects, animals, people, and even places. This task is to discover what the symbol means to you, in your own unique and ever-evolving personal dictionary, and the key to discovering your personal definitions of these symbols is to pay attention to the feelings that they conjure up in you.

Just as Freud pointed out, the symbols in your dreams very often come from something you saw or heard the day before you had the dream. Example: you watched CNN as you were falling asleep and you saw images of war. Don't you know the following morning you woke with a dream about killing and war! There you are, chalking it up to the TV you watched last night. Yes, it explains how the symbol originally arrived in the dream, but after forty-five years of studying and working with dreams, I hope you will trust me when I tell you that no matter what shows you watched before bed, your very sophisticated subconscious mind does not choose to dream of wars and killing unless it fits what you are trying to say to yourself. If there's no "battle" going on in your life this week, inner or outer, you won't choose the image of war. You'll choose something else.

Danny's Giraffe Dream

I was watching a CNN news report alerting the public
that a giraffe had escaped from the local zoo. The story
featured a computer-generated giraffe moving rather than a
film.

*LONG NECK
AWE - EXCITEMENT
SO BIG!*

There was a map of Chicago in the background. Other
people were in the room. I don't know who.

*SHOWS YOU WHERE PLACES
ARE+ HOW TO GET THERE*

In the next scene I was at my mother's house. I got up
and walked into the washroom. When I opened the door, to
my amazement right there in the bathtub as big as life itself
was the missing giraffe! I was shocked and in a complete
panic.

*CARING, CONCERNED
LOVING, HELPFUL*

Not wanting to alarm the giraffe, I backed away slowly
and closed the door. I immediately headed to the kitchen to
call 911. I told them my name and gave my address,
explaining I have the giraffe.

HELP

In the next scene, I was sitting at my mom's kitchen
table with the anchor from CNN. She had piles of books
around her and was looking up something in one book and
then going to another. She's heavy set, wearing a track suit,
and not very attractive looking.

NEWS

Suddenly the bathroom door opened and my wife's
cousin walked out, saying, "Hi you guys! How are you?"

FAMILY

FAMILY MEMBER

15

After circling the symbols in the dream description, ask yourself a few things that come to mind about each symbol, jotting these down next to the appropriate one. You can describe the image in detail, as if to a child or a person who has never seen it, noting what it looks like and what it does in the dream. Gayle Delaney would ask you to describe the symbol as if to an alien who has never seen or heard of that symbol. She would say, "Define the church. What is a church? What is its function?"

If the symbol is a person, ask yourself for two or three things that come to mind when you think about that person. Is she shy or straightforward, or especially kind or selfish? Sometimes a person brings to mind an incident, such as a shopping trip or an argument, rather than an adjective. Write everything down uncensored, and do not try too hard to figure out the symbol's meaning if it does not come to you right away. This is a good place to try Freud's technique of free association, saying whatever words or associations pop into your head when you think of a person, place, or object from your dream. As we said before, free association can bring you back to your own unique filing cabinet for your dream symbols, saying what they mean to you.

For example, Gerry dreamed of a huge church that is in the same neighborhood as the house he grew up in. Located on a busy street, the church is a major landmark in his city. When considering this symbol he remembered his childhood, when he was not allowed to visit this church himself. Being Jewish, the immense landmark held fascination and curiosity about the unknown for Gerry. It represented something illusory, something he longed to see but where he sensed he didn't belong.

When we look for the situation in the dreamer's life addressed by the dream, we can look at the symbols in the dream and ask: Does your experience with the symbol in the dream remind you of any similar experience in waking life recently? If the dreamer has associated a symbol with a feeling, a good question might be whether some recent experience or situation from the dreamer's life gives the dreamer the same feeling. Let's go back to Gerry and his church dream. Because of the feelings Gerry associated with this church, I asked: What is making you feel fascinated and curious now? Is there anything or anyone that seems illusory? Unreachable? Is there some situation in which you feel you don't quite belong? Some area you feel you are not allowed to go?

In considering these questions Gerry found the mirror. Notice why it is so important to listen to the language the dreamer uses: Gerry has been married to his childhood sweetheart for thirty years. She is the only person he has ever had a sexual experience with. While he is happily married and faithful (notice the play on words) and would not consider cheating on his wife, the new receptionist in his office has been sparking fascinating thoughts in Gerry's mind. The thought of having sex with another woman contributes to the same feelings that he had as a child living near a church he longed to see but "wasn't allowed to stray to" as it was "too far away from home." He felt he didn't "belong" there.

Note that Gerry's dream wasn't really about churches, even though the church was the symbol in his dream. The technique of free association can seem to carry you far from the original dream, but it can help you hook into your own personal meanings for the symbols. Say I am having an issue with my husband, Andy. He doesn't necessarily appear in my dream. If you were able to actually see the images in my personal database or filing cabinet and looked up Andy there, you would find my late first husband Murray there too, because he was also my husband. You would also find every boyfriend I have ever had! In fact, my late father, who was a male family member I sometimes felt dominated by, and who from time to time also had difficulty hearing me, appears in my list of associations with Andy.

If in a dream I am processing an issue I'm having with Andy this week, where I feel like I don't have a voice, my unconscious could choose one of those relationships from my past who appear in my list of associations with Andy and who also made me feel the same way in which Andy is making me feel today.

This shows the importance of analyzing the characters in a dream using different approaches, because characters are often an important symbol. We can ask: Who is this person? Where do I know him from? What are his character traits? Is she selfish? Giving? Assertive? Shy? What comes to my mind when I think of her? Who in my life this week has been behaving in a similar way? Is it I who have been behaving this way?

3. Play on Words and Puns

Though dream decoding can be done alone, you may find it helpful to work with a partner because describing things aloud can help you click more easily on a dream's meaning. (Even if you are working alone, you may find it helpful to talk out loud.)

The same as we do in our waking life, we constantly use play on words and puns in our dreaming minds. So if in conversation you use language like, "I was so embarrassed I thought I was going to die," you might dream that you are dying and it won't be that you are actually dying! It will simply be a case of your words appearing in the form of a metaphor. I often hear clients, in describing their dream say something like, "I was in a bathroom and I was stuck in a stall." This description from a dreamer begs the following question from me. "Is there anything you are stalling about in your current situation?"

Here's another example, in what I call my "Kneeling Dreams." In this series of dreams I was literally walking around on my knees. While recounting the dream to my husband I said, "I couldn't stand up." He responded by asking, "Why? Whom are you having trouble standing up to?" I realized immediately that the image was an accurate metaphor for my having difficulty standing up to someone!

My husband's question shows how a dreamer's play on words can provide the clue to the real-life situation. Andy asked what situation happened recently that made me feel like I couldn't stand up, or if there was someone I was having trouble standing up to. In another case one of my daughters dreamed she had three weeks to live. When I heard her say, "I thought I was going to die!" I asked her "Has anything happened lately that's making you feel like you're going to die?" The trick is to repeat the same expression the dreamer used while describing the dream and ask: What do you think happened recently that mirrors the expression you used in describing your dream?

4. The Action

Notice the action in the dream, putting a square around each action—or non-action—that takes place. I started running and I felt stuck and couldn't move. That's an example of an "action/non-action" point of entry. What are you, the dreamer, doing in the dream? Are you in the action, or outside the action, observing? What are other dream-characters doing? Write any comments or associations you have about the actions in a side column or alongside the action noted.

The actions in a dream could give you the clue to your waking situation that the dream is addressing. Can't run? You might ask what is going on in your life that is making you feel like you "can't run away from" it. Conversely maybe there something going on in your life that you have been running away from that your higher self doesn't want you to run from! You might phrase a third question by asking, "Is any situation making me feel stuck?"

Did you dream that you can't speak or that you are speaking but no sound is coming out? What do you think is making you feel like you "can't speak up" or are afraid to speak? Or is there a situation in which you feel like you aren't being heard by someone? Maybe in your dream you can't hear. Is there someone in your life who is telling you or trying to tell you something you just don't want to hear? What if you're hearing about something but don't feel like you understand what you are hearing? Maybe there is a situation you are having trouble relating to.

Here's another example of dream-action. Say you are not actually in the dream but more observing the action. In this case, you can come outside the dream and think about what situation in your life over the last few days you've observed. One client dreamed about a plane crashing next door to her house. She wasn't inside the plane. She was watching it. She used the crashing plane as a metaphor for a person she knows whose life was going downhill (there's the direction), and who also was coming to crash at her house. This is a great example of action in the dream, while at the same time the dreamer used play on words. It is a case of our sophisticated subconscious mind multi-tasking. You will find this phenomenon over and over again while decoding dreams.

Danny's Giraffe Dream

I was watching a CNN news report alerting the public that a giraffe had escaped from the local zoo. The story featured a computer-generated giraffe moving rather than a film.

There was a map of Chicago in the background. Other people were in the room. I don't know who.

In the next scene I was at my mother's house. I got up and walked into the washroom. When I opened the door, to my amazement right there in the bathtub as big as life itself was the missing giraffe! I was shocked and in a complete panic.

Not wanting to alarm the giraffe, I backed away slowly and closed the door. I immediately headed to the kitchen to call 911. I told them my name and gave my address, explaining I have the giraffe.

In the next scene, I was sitting at my mom's kitchen table with the anchor from CNN. She had piles of books around her and was looking up something in one book and then going to another. She's heavy set, wearing a track suit, and not very attractive looking.

Suddenly the bathroom door opened and my wife's cousin walked out, saying, "Hi you guys! How are you?"

5. The Plot

If the points of entry so far haven't helped you click on the situation the dream is mirroring, try the plot. This is exactly the same as what we learned in English class back in high school. What is the story behind the story? Look at what actually happens in the dream and see what situation in your waking life this week is similar.

This point of entry worked for Grace, who dreamed she was driving her car. In the dream she changed lanes without turning on her signal light and was stopped by a policeman who gave her a ticket for $118.00. We identified two plot lines, or stories behind the story of this dream: a change in direction, and a situation where there was a huge price to pay. As it turns out, both these story lines resonated with Grace who immediately identified her waking life situation: she was about to change her major without having consulted anyone about her decision. There was the mirror about changing lanes with no signal light. A wrong decision in this case could potentially carry a high price.

Another example of a dream plot comes from my daughter's "three weeks to live" dream. As I mentioned before, she dreamed she had three weeks to live, and moreover, in her dream she claimed I was unable to help her. The next morning we solved the puzzle of the dream by discovering that her exams were beginning in three weeks. Of course I wasn't able to help her in the dream—I was unable to help in waking life! Here was a dream where the plot that I could not help her, combined with the symbol of three weeks and the play on words where she felt like she was "going to die," all came together to mirror exactly how she felt coming up to her exams.

6. Repetition

Remember read it, write it, recite it? It's one way we learn. We get it when it's repeated. The unconscious mind uses repetition all the time in dreams. That way if we didn't get the message the first time, we see it again, but it comes to us in a different way each time.

Danny's Giraffe Dream

AWE X2
FAMILY MEMBER X3
HELP X4

LONG NECK — AWE = ②
AWE = EXCITEMENT
SO BIG!

INTERESTED

I was watching a CNN news report alerting the public that a giraffe had escaped from the local zoo. The story featured a computer-generated giraffe moving rather than a film.

There was a map of Chicago in the background. Other people were in the room. I don't know who.

SHOWS YOU WHERE PLACES ARE+ HOW TO GET THERE — HELP = ①

CARING, CONCERNED LOVING, HELPFUL

SHOCKED-AMAZED
AWE + PANIC
AWE = ①

In the next scene I was at my mother's house. I got up and walked into the washroom. When I opened the door, to my amazement right there in the bathtub as big as life itself was the missing giraffe! I was shocked and in a complete panic.

HELP = ②
FAMILY MEMBER = ①

CAUTIOUS

Not wanting to alarm the giraffe, I backed away slowly and closed the door. I immediately headed to the kitchen to call 911. I told them my name and gave my address, explaining I have the giraffe.

HELP = ③

COMPLETE SURPRISE HOW SHE APPEARS FROM NOWHERE AS IF SHE BELONGS

In the next scene, I was sitting at my mom's kitchen table with the anchor from CNN. She had piles of books around her and was looking up something in one book and then going to another. She's heavy set, wearing a track suit, and not very attractive looking.

Suddenly the bathroom door opened and my wife's cousin walked out, saying, "Hi you guys! How are you?"

NEWS

HELP = ④

FAMILY
FAMILY MEMBER = ②

FAMILY MEMBER = ③

22

There are many ways our dreams repeat things to make sure we get the message. This happened to me when my first book came out and I was invited to appear on TV in New York. While I had plenty of experience speaking on radio, television was new for me. One night shortly before my trip to New York, I dreamed of a ghost. What does that mean in my personal vocabulary of associations? It means I am scared. Later in the same dream, I was standing on the abyss of a cliff. What does that mean in my personal vocabulary of associations? It also means I am scared! And close to morning as I was waking I dreamed about my grade five teacher. What does this sight mean to me? It means I am scared!! The three completely different symbols, once decoded, are an example of repetition. It is my saying to myself, "I'm scared. I'm scared. I'm scared." And the question I was able to ask myself upon decoding the images was, "What am I feeling frightened about?"

When we analyze our dreams, we often find the same message repeated using multiple symbols. We might also learn that multiple points of entry guide us to the same situation, like my daughter discovered in her "three weeks to live" dream. Again, this happened to me when one of my "kneeling" dreams took place in the office of a man named Neil! Apart from the multiple play on words ("kneeling" in "Neil's" office), Neil is a friend and associate of my brother so this character led me right to the person I was having trouble standing up to. Neil's appearance in my dream linked me to my brother.

Repetition in A Dream Map

Here's what repetition looks like when you create it on a dream map. I am posting Annie's Have Faith Dream map here not for its analysis but rather to illustrate to you how, even if we don't know the dreamer or anything about her current situation, you can still see something taking shape just by deconstructing her associations to the people and places in the dream. I chose a dream with plenty of repetition so you can see how sophisticated the unconscious is in choosing its metaphors.

The dreamer was discussing a matter that had to do with her family. How did we discover that? Annie was at a lake house in the dream that reminded her of her family's house. The dreamer references "family" a second time when she gives a man at the house a packet of papers and she associates the man as being a doctor like her father. Annie says family to herself a third time in her being "at a big family wedding." The fourth time the dreamer says family to herself she places her brother Stan in the dream. The repetition even continues a fifth and sixth time towards the end of the dream, referring again to her family's lake home and to her friend Shawna, whom the dreamer also associates with family time in Michigan. We found another round of repetition in this dream about writing. We see it the first time when she Xeroxes and collates papers, a task Annie associates with her writing group. The second time, she refers to writing by the appearance of her poet friend into the dream, and a third time when she mentions her physical therapist, who, also happens to be the co-author of Annie's book. The repetition continues a fourth time when her old book editor appears in the dream. There are two more cases of repetition in Annie's dream. This time it's not so much who the issue is with or what the dream is addressing. Now, the dreamer helps herself get in touch with her feelings by presenting situations or a plot that make her feel uncomfortable, over and over. She feels discomfort because the man (doctor) she gives the papers to, is annoyed with her. She feels uncomfortable again at the thought of an ex-friend of hers seeing the dreamer with her brother (who is overweight) and mistakenly thinking it's her husband. The dreamer creates a third scenario in which she feels discomfort, when her friend gets "mad" at her for asking if she has seen a doctor yet. The fourth discomfort comes via Annie's associations seen in her description of her poet friend having rejected her poetry. Finally, we see Annie refer to her co-author having received kudos, which caused the dreamer to feel slighted, hence, some discomfort.

In her waking life situation, this dream involved a family member criticizing a recent work of Annie's, and how the criticism made her feel. Thankfully, this dreamer uses the function of repetition to direct herself to the aspect of her personality she needs at this particular time in her specific situation. That solution is to be in touch with her self-confidence. This is a time to reach inside to the part of Annie that can build herself up, and have some faith, as opposed to feeling uncomfortable. Annie accomplishes this by bringing three characters into the dream who she associates as being very self-confident: her brother, her poet friend, and her old book editor.

Annie's Have Faith Dream

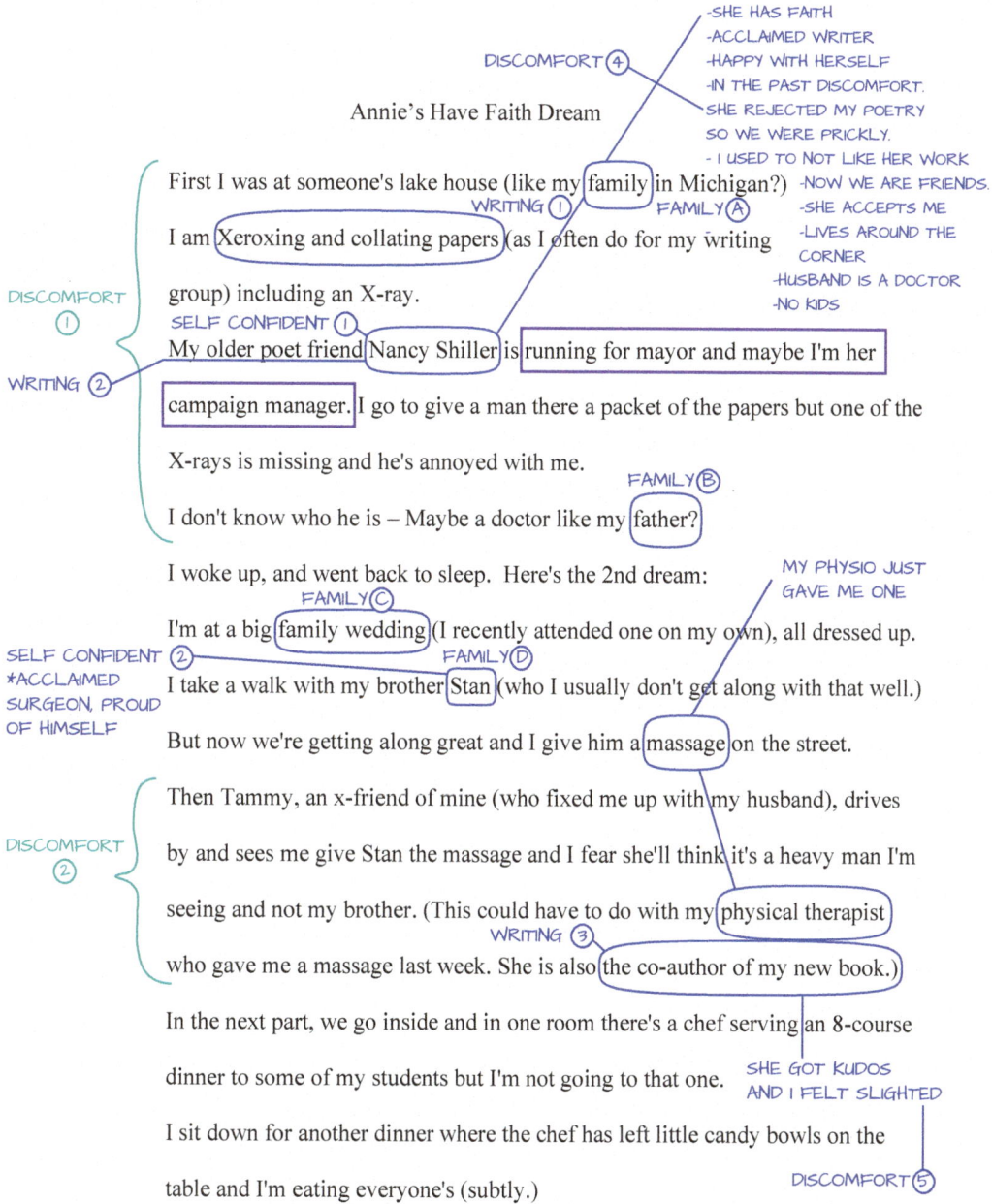

DISCOMFORT ④

-SHE HAS FAITH
-ACCLAIMED WRITER
-HAPPY WITH HERSELF
-IN THE PAST DISCOMFORT.
SHE REJECTED MY POETRY
SO WE WERE PRICKLY.
- I USED TO NOT LIKE HER WORK
-NOW WE ARE FRIENDS.
-SHE ACCEPTS ME
-LIVES AROUND THE
CORNER
-HUSBAND IS A DOCTOR
-NO KIDS

First I was at someone's lake house (like my family in Michigan?)

WRITING ①   FAMILY Ⓐ

I am Xeroxing and collating papers (as I often do for my writing

DISCOMFORT
①

group) including an X-ray.

SELF CONFIDENT ①

WRITING ②

My older poet friend Nancy Shiller is running for mayor and maybe I'm her

campaign manager. I go to give a man there a packet of the papers but one of the

X-rays is missing and he's annoyed with me.

FAMILY Ⓑ

I don't know who he is – Maybe a doctor like my father?

I woke up, and went back to sleep. Here's the 2nd dream:

FAMILY Ⓒ

I'm at a big family wedding (I recently attended one on my own), all dressed up.

SELF CONFIDENT ②
*ACCLAIMED
SURGEON, PROUD
OF HIMSELF

FAMILY Ⓓ

I take a walk with my brother Stan (who I usually don't get along with that well.)

But now we're getting along great and I give him a massage on the street.

MY PHYSIO JUST
GAVE ME ONE

Then Tammy, an x-friend of mine (who fixed me up with my husband), drives

DISCOMFORT
②

by and sees me give Stan the massage and I fear she'll think it's a heavy man I'm

seeing and not my brother. (This could have to do with my physical therapist

WRITING ③

who gave me a massage last week. She is also the co-author of my new book.)

In the next part, we go inside and in one room there's a chef serving an 8-course

dinner to some of my students but I'm not going to that one.

SHE GOT KUDOS
AND I FELT SLIGHTED

I sit down for another dinner where the chef has left little candy bowls on the

table and I'm eating everyone's (subtly.)

DISCOMFORT ⑤

SELF CONFIDENT ③

I'm sitting one seat away from Kate Wilson, my old book editor. Kate runs

WRITING ④

marathons. I fixed her up with her husband.

After 6 months of marriage, she is complaining that she's not pregnant yet.

I tell her I saw her marathon picture on Facebook and ask if she's seen a fertility

doctor yet.

I tell her a fertility doctor might tell her to stop running.

DISCOMFORT
③

She gets very mad at me and says I shouldn't treat friends like patients or pills.

FAMILY Ⓔ+Ⓕ

My old close Michigan friend Shawna - (who I saw on Hanukah & who has two

kids) hears me and gets offended that I somehow spilled that she went to a

fertility doctor.

I defend myself and say "But I wanted you to get pregnant and have the babies."

Then I go to the bathroom and a female student of mine wants to go too, but I get

there first. Then we all leave…

• FAMILY 6X
• DISCOMFORT 5X
• WRITING 4X
_____

SOLUTIONS
1) SELF CONFIDENCE X3
2) FAITH
3) ACTION= GETS THERE FIRST!
       = FEELS OKAY ABOUT
       GETTING THERE FIRST.
    GREAT METAPHOR TO END WITH!

Note on Self Regulating

While in our conscious life we are natural avoiders and deniers, we are at the same time self-regulating organisms. In other words, whatever we may be under-reacting to in waking life, the dream is going to over-react; hence the nightmare and/or recurring dreams/repetition.

a) The nightmare or recurring message is the over-reaction that creates the balance to your under-reaction. Jung called it compensation.

b) The successful over-reaction will grab your attention to look at something you have been avoiding in waking life and therefore inspire you. As Adler described, a strong emotion in your dreams propels you to expand your habitual responses or Lifestyle.

Among other helpful changes, these dream experiences increase the possibility that you'll bring up the subject with a friend or family member. In our human tendency of avoiding situations, holding back emotions or keeping in what we want to say, we are figuratively filling up a balloon. The great news is once you are engaged in discussion about a subject you are, in essence, letting air out of that balloon and the process of regulating has begun.

Another benefit that comes from discussing with others is you get feedback about what the images might mean. It starts you thinking. Discussion helps you come out of your own head about the issue you are attempting to problem-solve. Truth is there is nothing better than brainstorming with others to help widen your scope of ideas, not only for what the dream may be about but what options it presents for solutions!

When I had repeating images that once decoded meant, "I'm scared. I'm scared. I'm scared," it was the over-reaction to the feelings of tension and fear I was not expressing in daylight. The nightmares spurred me to decode the meaning and ultimately prodded me to discuss my worry aloud during the day.

The Lesson: Don't be necessarily looking for the "exact" mirror when trying the points of entry. If you are very sad in the dream, try looking for a situation that's been making you feel a little sad.

Dream analysis is the art of puzzle solving. It is an interactive experience and always best if you have a full bag of puzzle pieces to try. I am giving you notes as opposed to rigid rules for decoding dreams. My hope and intention is to give you plenty of pieces to try, so if one doesn't fit there are more in the bag.

CHAPTER TWO: SOLUTION-FINDING IN DREAM ANALYSIS

O n the subject of finding solutions to our problems, I must impress upon you how I see it. In my view there is no such thing as a "right way" or a "wrong way," a "good way" or a "bad way" to approach life's difficulties. For me it is more a matter of "appropriate" or "inappropriate." Does your reaction fit the situation at hand? I believe dreams point us to the reaction or behavior that is the appropriate response, even when it is not a reaction we are accustomed to or necessarily comfortable with! Decoded dreams give us the opportunity to practice unexercised aspects of our personality.

Solution-Finding Points of Entry

1. Direct Solution

Sometimes the dream makes life easy for you and gives you a direct solution to the problem. Elias Howe, the inventor of the sewing machine was stuck trying to find a way to work the needle when he had a dream of being captured by lance-carrying cannibals who put him in a pot of boiling water. When he tried to escape, the cannibals stopped him by poking their spears. Howe remembered looking down at the spears in the dream to discover each had a hole in the tip. Where before the dream he had the hole for the thread at the top of the needle, upon waking he had found the solution in placing the hole at the tip instead. The sewing machine was invented!

2. Take The Dream Story Outside to Waking Life

More often than the story of Elias Howe's dream, the solution to the problem is not so direct. One way to find a solution is to take the actual story of the dream (even if it seems unrealistic) and treat it as if it happened in waking life. Ask yourself what you would do if such a thing happened.

One client, Sherri, described losing her husband in a market place. One minute he was there and the next minute he was gone. In the dream she is racing around calling his name, searching everywhere but to no avail.

I asked her, "If that happened in waking life, what would you really do?" She said "The same! I would be running around calling his name and looking for him." I inquired, "Wouldn't you stop and ask for help at some point? Maybe go to the administration and ask them to call him on a loud speaker or help you find him?"

A truck driver by trade, Sherri's husband was leaving on a long trip in bad weather with more storms forecast. She feared something might happen to him and she would be left alone…"losing him." The problem was how Sherri was not discussing her fears about losing her husband and being alone. She was holding everything in. This is an example of self-regulating. Sherri is feeling very emotional and yet is not discussing her deepest fear with anyone. The dream plays out her fear.

Taking the dream situation outside the dream and considering what measures you would take in waking life is a great way to find the solution to the issue. In this case it was asking for help! Speaking up about her fear to someone released Sherri's pent up worries and helped let some air out of the balloon that created the nightmare.

3. The Action

Working with the action in the dream is similar to taking the story outside to waking life, except in this case you can also work with the dream as it is.

When I work with the action in the dream, my question is often, "Is the action the dreamer is taking appropriate to the dream situation?" For example, in The Picnic Dream I cited earlier, the ants at a picnic are everywhere and the dreamer is trying to push them away with her hands. This remedy is sadly not working in the dream as it would fail too if tried in waking life. The response is simply inappropriate; ineffective. The dreamer's life situation of an affair gone sour leads her to reassess her reaction and its appropriateness. In this case the dreamer was considering ending the affair but had not taken the steps needed to end the relationship. Her ineffective action is mirrored in the dream. Looking at the dream as it was, I suggested she might "get some Raid." The dream helped her take a more effective approach and soon after, she did end the relationship.

How about cases where you take the role of an observer in the dream? Would you find it more appropriate in the scenario to be involved in the action of the dream instead? Once you have uncovered the situation the dream is addressing, it might be pointing you to be "involved in," as opposed to "removed from," your current life's issue.

4. Jung's Active Imagination

Active imagination is the act of changing the dream by using your imagination. In doing so you are changing your mind, same as if you go downtown to buy a shirt and then see a pair of shoes in a window and decide to buy them instead of the shirt.

You can use active imagination inside or outside the dream. Here's an example. A child described his nightmare to his mother. He said, "There was a giant coming after me in my dream!" His mom, treating the dream as if in the present tense said, "I'm coming into that dream with you and we are building a wall so tall the giant can't get over it!" By way of active imagination the parent put herself in the dream with her son and at the same time solved the problem about conquering the giant.

This at once gave the child confidence and protection. Engaging a child with a response like this also expands his ability to problem solve creatively.

Another example you may have heard is how lucid dreamers can stop running away in their dreams and turn to face their pursuer. You don't have to be lucid in a dream to accomplish this suggestion. You can do so after you are awake by imagining a different ending! Just like the parent who enters the dream to escape the giant, by the simple act of imagining you have begun the visual process of changing your mind.

5. Symbols, Metaphors and Characters (A Gestalt Approach)

When using a character as a point of entry to decode your dream, I have suggested you think of two or three things you associate with that person. Is she shy or straightforward, or especially kind or selfish? Sometimes a person brings to mind an incident, such as a shopping trip or an argument, rather than an adjective. Do the same if you are investigating an animal.

I have found again and again it is no accident that you choose certain symbols to appear in your dream. The unconscious is very sophisticated and can multitask. You can use a symbol to help you uncover why you had that dream last night, but later in looking for a solution the same symbol might serve another purpose altogether. You might find the symbol gives you the opportunity to "rehearse," or practice a behavior you need in waking life.

Earlier in this workbook, I asked you to think about a recent situation in which anyone (not necessarily the actual characters from the dream) behaved similarly to the way you described the people in the dream. This can work for dream animals too.

One of my favorite examples comes from one of my lovely daughters, who, years ago, was dreaming about cats. Her associations to cats are simple and still hold true today. She loves them so much and only wishes to get close, but unfortunately she must keep her distance because she is highly allergic. At the time of her cat dreams, she was dating a fellow who she thought she loved but knew deep down inside that he wasn't a good match. The message was not to get too close. Like we see in this dream, the unconscious is always more ready to present the truth than our conscious mind is!

I often use the example of a cat when lecturing. It is fun to choose three or four people in the room to hear all their different associations. It helps me impress upon everyone how unique our filing cabinet of associations is.

Here is my own personal example of a cat dream. I want to take a quick detour and describe some aspects of my past so you see the story I'm going to tell in its right context. In my family of origin we were four children. My eldest sister is fifteen years my senior. I was four years old when she married. My second sister is ten years older than me and I was eight when she married. The two sisters were close and understandably, I was not really included in their conversations. Now add two more facts. There were only 20 years or so difference between their age and my mom, where it was closer to a 40-year stretch for me. From where I stood as a young child, it seemed like my mother was my mom, but my sisters' friend. You won't be surprised to learn I grew up with inclusion issues.

In the Introduction, you'll remember how I discuss Freud's theory that our current experiences open a file from our memory, which gives us our initial reaction. Hence my tendency to jump to the conclusion that someone is "excluding me." As Freud explained, we actually attract people and situations in order to recreate our childhood experience. Freud called it repetition compulsion. We recreate these experiences, even though sometimes negative or harmful, because this is what connects us to our identity. It is how we have come to see ourselves. All that said, here's my cat dream story.

One time an acquaintance of mine (who I thought was a friend), behaved annoyingly cool and disconnected towards me in a restaurant. That night I had what I call my cat dream. Quite different from my daughter, I find cats aloof, snobby and independent. I don't particularly like them. When I asked myself who in my life had been behaving in a similar way, the incident with that girlfriend came to light. In fact once I started mulling over my relationship with her I realized that I always initiated our get-togethers.

From this dream we see how my associations with the symbol "cat" helped me uncover the situation that was bothering me. Here´s the thing. In looking for solutions in this dream, I realized I needed to emulate this symbol in my current situation. I was chasing after a relationship in which I was not being treated nicely, so I needed to become like the cat, behaving in an independent, cool and disconnected way. The cat as a solution helped me distance myself from that person.

While this kind of behavior felt foreign to me, it was also an opportunity to exercise what Frederick Perls referred to as the "disowned" or "under-invested" aspects of my personality. Perls might have asked me to become the cat. Carl Jung would ask the dreamer to try and move closer to her Shadow, that aspect of the dream that makes her feel the most uncomfortable. It's the same principal, said a different way. If you are uncomfortable with the characteristics of a symbol, try to "become" like that symbol. In doing so you are stretching yourself. You are opening up your possibilities about how to respond to your current situation. You become more flexible.

What does "becoming" the cat look like? You start by having an actual conversation, speaking out loud as the cat. In order to use a Gestalt point of entry and speak as the character, you will have to toss your discomfort aside and pretend you are an actor doing improvisation. In this conversation between me and the cat, here's what my improvisation looks like.

Layne: I don't like you because you walk by me like you think you are above everyone else. You're a snob.

The cat: Oh. I'm not a snob! I'm just focused on taking care of business. If I am hungry, getting some food would be first on my mind. There would be no time for chatting. It's not how I operate.

Layne: Well to me you're arrogant and disconnected. Like the few times in my life I had experiences with you it's more been a case of my trying to get you to sit on my lap so I can pat you and you'll walk away, never even bothering to acknowledge me!

The cat: It's not like that at all. It's not a case of me wanting to snub you. It's more a case of my not functioning the same way as you do. I'm wired differently. I'm not like a dog, most of whom will jump into your arms. I prefer being alone. Patting and hugging just don't feel right for me. But I would feel that way towards any situation or person. I'm most comfortable sticking to myself.

Layne: Well, I'm more like how you describe the dog, so behaving like you seems hurtful to me.

The cat: That's the most important thing. I am who I am. This is how I operate. It's no offense to you.

The process of having this conversation provides a few important insights for me, the dreamer. Up to now, I have used the cat symbol to point me towards the situation I was thinking about when I had the dream. The cat conversation is especially rich though, because it comes from me personally. I am the one who opens my mind to show that the cat's intention was never to reject me. This in turn opens the possibility of seeing the woman who I associated with a cat as "just like that." Maybe she is simply the kind of person whose style, like the cat, is to keep to herself. It's not her natural way to initiate.

As for me "becoming" like a cat in my response to this woman in future, let me begin by saying the following.

When you are striving for a lasting change in your life, the surest way to succeed is to approach change from a loving and relaxed place. Similarly, the surest way to fail is to come at it from a place of anger or dislike, or worse hate.

Filling yourself with anger doesn't move you away from someone. For that matter, it will block any real change inside yourself! The best example I can think of is the emotional thrashing people give themselves when they go off a diet. They slip, they curse themselves, and they head right back to the fridge. In my case, I didn't want to hold on to my initial, angry reaction of feeling rejected by this woman as a springboard for my new "cool, cat-like" behavior.

No. In order to truly become the cat and re-own my Shadowed "cool" traits I have to eliminate my anger. The following formula does not happen overnight, but I assure you time and practice do make real change possible. So, the first task was to attach my feeling "excluded" to where it rightfully belongs, to my childhood experience; to my sisters. Next I needed to revisit my childhood, but this time through the eyes of me, the adult. Seeing it as I do now, of course I didn't "deserve" to be left out! It only happened because of the big age difference between us!

Keeping this adult perspective while reviewing my conversation with the cat, I can accept that my assumption of being snubbed was incorrect, both in the case of my sisters and the girlfriend. If the woman in the restaurant did not reject me, there is suddenly no anger there. Not from me and not from her. I must respect the conversation I had with the cat. Now, even if I don't like that behavior, I can very simply accept the woman for who she is with no expectation of her changing.

What happens when you accept a person at face value, exactly as they are, and remove any expectations that they will change? I call it true love. This for me is somehow connected to how we come into and leave this world alone, how we each travel on our own path. In other words, we all respond and treat others based on the framework of our own, unique life experience. This understanding removes you from thinking someone did something "to you." You are not the victim. You have not been rejected. If you appreciate instead how this person is on her own life's path, her decisions and her behavior all based on her personal whole life experience, you remove your victim stance.

This exercise is less about anger aimed outwards at someone, and more about treating yourself with the kindness and respect necessary in order to make decisions about your relationships. It is the difference between love for yourself and anger for the other. Here is what happened. Not overnight, but over some years. This experience and this dream marked the beginning of a decision to distinguish between my friends and my acquaintances. Today, when I feel excluded (my knee jerk response) I stop to look at each experience on a case-by-case basis. I accept that my acquaintances may treat me in a "cat-like" way, so I experience no disappointment or anger. Likewise, I'm able to separate from them and treat them in a slightly cooler, more "cat-like" manner. At the same time, I have slowly gravitated towards friends who share my "dog-like" qualities.

Another benefit to embracing the cat as "a part of me" was connecting to how I like being by myself. In short, if I am appreciating my time alone, it's not in my viewfinder who is initiating a get-together. On the contrary, these days, it is often me hoping no one notices me so I can sit alone!!

For me personally, and this was after all, my dream, the goal is to exercise the Shadow cat part of my personality; my more independent, comfortable-with-myself side. It is the opposite of my more familiar who-is-calling-me, am-I-being-included side. If I am as comfortable in my own skin as the cat, I won't be focused on receiving goodies from outside myself. And so, a good and lasting lesson from a cat I thought I hated, and who I now embrace!

Be warned! As I explained earlier, we have many disowned parts. But all of our personality together, the parts we acknowledge and those we don't, are our potential. And all these parts of us appear in our dreams. Like the example of my needing to access the "cat" potential in me, all the parts of you too are there for the taking. Literally.

Here's one more dream-character who points towards an underinvested aspect of the dreamer's potential. You will remember in the Introduction, I discussed how the people who bring us up send us messages, which reinforce that it is better to be one way than another. Well, one of my teachers described her upbringing in a home with siblings. Like many other children in this situation she learned that being selfish isn't okay, often hearing her mom say sentences like, "Go look after your brother," and "Share your toys!" The messages she received helped her put that aspect of her personality to sleep; it is an under-invested aspect of her Self.

So she was taught to share, share, share and do, do, do. She was over-invested in saying yes when asked to do something. When she was forty and just home from the hospital after surgery, a colleague asked her to work on some documents while she was recuperating at home. Considering how she was feeling at the time the appropriate response would have been to say no, but my teacher found herself agreeing to look over the work.

That night she dreamed about Jennifer, a girl she knew in college seventeen years earlier. Having full knowledge and experience with dream analysis, she asked herself what the heck Jennifer was doing in her dream! She hadn't seen her in almost twenty years. My teacher asked herself, "What are the first few things that come to my mind when I think of her?" The answer? "She was such a selfish girl!"

This was precisely the approach my teacher needed as a solution to her current situation. While she may have been disconnected from her ability to behave selfishly, her unconscious mind brought Jennifer into the dream so she could reach towards that personality trait as the appropriate response to a colleague who asked her to work only a day after her release from the hospital.

Now, when a person with a certain character trait appears in your dream, I am not saying you are going to "become" that person. My teacher didn't suddenly become relaxed and ready to tell her co-worker how she really felt about looking over documents. No. I am saying this character's appearance in your dream points you to the solution to the problem. Please be aware too that your filing cabinet is going to push open and play that same CD every time you try something that goes against your initial response, which comes from the initial messages you received in your life. With your dreams, your unconscious is urging you to lean away from your first reaction and try something new. My teacher accomplished this, by going back to her colleague and explaining that she wanted to wait and see how her recovery went before making any commitments.

Rehearsing new behaviors is like exercising muscles for the first time in a gym. Underinvested character traits must be developed. At first, each time you work out you are sore for days. You are putting unfamiliar muscles to work and it feels strange.

After a time the movement comes easily and feels natural. The same thing happens with our behavior. Sometimes we begin practicing a new behavior in a dream. After a while, we bring the new behavior out of the dream scenes and exercise it in waking life. Before long, it feels comfortable. And with this newfound comfort, we gain flexibility and adaptability to the different situations we face. We become less predictable in our approach to solving life's problems; we increase our potential.

Now you are no longer stuck in your patterns, which may be appropriate in certain situations but work against you in others. Accepting all the different parts of your Self is what Carl Jung called individuation; Freud and Perls, maturation; and Edgar Cayce called it "the best self," or the soul.

6. Polarities

Look for opposing characters, situations, points of view, or emotions in your dream and they may point you towards solutions in your life. Freud proposed that the unconscious mind doesn't say "either, or," but instead inserts both opposing poles in the dream. When you see a polarity in your dream, you may want to investigate if the appropriate response to your current life situation is somewhere in the middle. It doesn't have to be "Either I'm going to do this, or I'm going to do that."

So if an incident happened in your waking life and you are silent when you need your voice, a silent personality and a very assertive personality might appear in your dream. In this scenario, the dreamer isn't going to respond with a confident assertiveness that is completely new to him. But the knowledge of the polarity can suggest a direction to reach for. Recognizing this polarity gives the dreamer an opportunity to exercise an underinvested aspect of his personality and use a little part of his voice at first. Using even a small voice is the first step in exercising that newfound part of yourself.

7. Self-Regulation

The idea of polarities brings me back to my Note on Self-Regulating from Chapter One. Self-regulating, or correcting the extremes of your response, may give you the solution to your waking life problem. Here's an example. Sandra was experiencing great sadness upon the loss of her grandmother a month previous. She was at the same time feeling resentful for the way she saw her mother treat her grandmother before she died. Sandra was neither expressing, nor even acknowledging her feelings.

Sandra dreamed her brother died and she was the only one who knew, leaving her in a position to have to tell her mother. Awake and crying, Sandra had to acknowledge her sadness and continuing feelings of upset with her mother. She couldn't keep repressing these feelings from herself and others. As a correction of Sandra's repression, her unconscious mind chose a very sad story in order to pry her emotions out into the open.

Sandra's grief in the dream, in which she had received very sad news that no one else knew, indicated the need to regulate her behavior by expressing her feelings. Another method, Take the Dream Story Outside to Waking Life, also pointed Sandra in the direction of expressing her feelings to her mother. They both led her to voice her disappointment to her mom about her behavior.

Life-Changing Solutions Using Deeper Points of Entry

8. Looking Back in The Mirror

When I was a child, I used to stand behind the door of my bathroom and arrange the mirror that hung on it to reflect into the mirror on the wall behind the door. That way I was able to see myself in a mirror that reflected another mirror, inside another mirror inside another mirror, and so on, far away into an unknown distance. It fascinated me, and actually still does today. This reflection of the same image has a kind of tunneling effect. In the same way, the issues we face in our current lives reflect familiar attitudes and feelings from our past.

Freud gave us the tools to use our dreams as a mirror to our childhood. As I described in the first part of this workbook, Freud's technique of free association brings us back to the relationships and feelings from our past that underlie our responses in the present. One common technique of free association is to pick a symbol or an image from your dream. Say the symbol to yourself or you can write it. For example, if there was a door in your dream, say the word door. Then let the next thought just pop into your head. See what that is. Just continue listening to each thought as it leads to the next. Another approach comes from Dr. Henry Reed, the former Director of Research at the Edgar Cayce Foundation. He advises you to lie back, close your eyes and think of a story from your childhood that makes you feel the same way as you felt in the dream.

"I'LL BARK, AND YOU BARK THE FIRST THING THAT COMES TO MIND."

Whether you focus on the symbols, the characters, the story or the emotions in the dream, the most important part of free association is to go with your first answer without judging whether it seems appropriate or sensible. If you do this, it will bring you back to the moments from your past when you set up your filing cabinet of automatic associations and responses to the situations in your life. Free association lets us see how we developed our habitual reactions to life's situations. When we see this, we can plan how to live and respond more flexibly.

Here is a quick example. Suppose your mother used to yell at you for spilling milk on the floor by accident. She spanked you for your clumsiness. At the age of four, you agreed with her. Her truth was your truth. Now, at forty, when you drop papers by accident at work, do you reprimand yourself with disgust at your clumsiness? Last night's dream may mirror the fact that you spilled papers on the floor at work yesterday and beat yourself up over it, but by going back to your childhood relationship with your mother, you can discover why you are so hard on yourself for this simple accident.

At forty, you have the option to reassess whether you think your mother was correct. Is a four-year-old incompetent for spilling milk? Today you may realize you have a different opinion than your mother did. If you finally understand where your harsh judgment of yourself originates, you can decide to change your opinion. Once you have done this exercise, maybe the first few times you drop papers on the floor your initial, knee-jerk reaction is still to curse yourself. I assure you though, after you understand where your judgments are coming from, you will start to catch yourself when you react this way. And like I explained about working out new muscles in a gym, after a while you will find it easy to say, "Oh, I dropped papers on the floor—no problem." You might even find yourself bending down and picking them up without attaching any blame at all.

By tracing the origin of your current reaction, you make sure your feelings really do belong to your current situation. For example, Henry is overcome with jealousy because he sees his second wife laughing with a business associate at a party. His second wife is very devoted to Henry, and he knows that. Yet this scene sparks a memory of what he felt fifteen years earlier when he discovered his first wife in an affair. Henry's emotional memory has kicked in. When you analyze your dream at this level you can tap into the origin of your response and evaluate if it is appropriate now. After realizing where his reaction comes from, Henry is likely to share his experiences with his second wife rather than scream at her. He can create a supportive relationship with her, rather than recreating the conflicts of his first marriage.

There is a bonus from this level of dreamwork. When you understand the origin of your judgments, you will recognize the messages you received in your childhood that caused you to reject aspects of yourself. Like my teacher and her Jennifer dream, which allowed her to say no, you can start to accept your disowned parts; to expand your Lifestyle, as Alfred Adler would have said. Our self-judgments and our disowned parts both come from the same source: the messages we received as children.

Even better, an expanded acceptance of ourselves, leads to a greater acceptance of others. It will become easier for you to embrace the positive qualities of those you love and forgive their faults. You will start to see that many feelings of anger or hatred towards others come from our lack of awareness that the same traits are in fact underdeveloped, rejected aspects of ourselves. And just as there are positive ways to incorporate our underinvested personality traits into our own life, there are also ways to be supportive of our loved ones' personal growth without assigning blame or judgment.

When you link reactions in your current life to situations from your childhood, you have the opportunity not only to re-assess the situation, but also to forgive. I hope you can always keep this in mind as you look back in the mirror. Now you are looking back as an adult. You can re-visit instances from your childhood and discover new emotions which might soon reside comfortably next to the ones you felt back then. And in a number of instances, you may find yourself more understanding of your parent's reactions when you look at them now. Many times, old wounds can become a new understanding and along with it forgiveness. If you can find some understanding and forgiveness through looking deeper into your dream, you can lift some of your old anger and feel lighter.

9. Finding Your Archetypes

We human beings all have and have always had many things in common. We share fears, wishes, desires, and needs; they are part of our common human destiny. We all pass through transitions, different stages of life. We each understand different rites of passage; our teen years, we rebel against authority. We mate. We date. We marry. We experience maturation, separation, sadness, loss, joy, love, excitement, and happiness.

But why would you want to focus on those elements inside you that are a part of our common humanity? For one thing, many people find value in realizing they are not alone in their experience. Dreams with a universal quality typically come during transitions, or at times of great stress, or uncertainty about moving forward towards individuation. It is precisely during these times that you might feel alone. Have you ever found yourself thinking that no one else has gone through what you are going through, or at least not in quite the same way? Knowing that others have gone through what you are going through helps sometimes, especially when you are feeling alone.

The things we have in common, it stands to reason, have appeared in stories since the beginning of humanity. And the images and themes from familiar stories show up in our dreams, the same way as they have in plays, movies, poems, and fables throughout time. There can be tremendous value in bringing these images and motifs to the forefront and seeing how they appear in our dreams.

Using this point of entry for solution-finding helps you hone your ability to connect with something familiar to you, because when you recognize the story or element you chose you are bound to discover a lesson. Your current experience can be enriched by looking at someone who went through a similar experience before you. How did that person respond to the situation?

When you identify with a powerful character or image in your dream, this can help you recognize a source of wisdom or strength in yourself. You might even find your dream reminds you of a story that ultimately prods you to rethink your position because you don't want to get caught like the person in the story! Previously I discussed how you put yourself in a more powerful position by re-assessing from an adult perspective the things you learned as a child. Often we change the opinions our parents had and then make new, adult decisions for ourselves. You may find yourself doing the same using this method, for here you will learn that our dreams bring shades of old stories and decisions that you can try to emulate, or change, as you like. Once you connect your story with a more universal theme, you can assess if you want to gather strength from the characters by behaving just as they did, or gather strength because you are making the decision not to follow the same path!

Direct Association

As we saw in the first section of this workbook, Carl Gustav Jung sought to connect our dreams with the archetypes experienced by humans across generations. Jung called this process amplification and described the tool of direct association to make it happen. This is what you do. Break the dream down, the same way we did when attempting to decode the dream with a dream map. But instead of isolating a symbol in order to determine its meaning, let's isolate a picture, an action, or a motif. Jung worked with images and events.

The first part is very similar to the process of connecting your dream to your own past. But instead of asking yourself questions like, "Do any of my associations here seem familiar?" or "Does anyone in the dream spark a memory of someone from my past?" or maybe, "When have I felt this way before in my life?" you ask yourself what story from a book, a movie, a television show, a fairy tale, a bible story, or any story you know reminds you of your dream. You can also choose a part of the dream to explore this way. Think about the symbol or character. Just like in free association, let a story or person from a story pop into your head. See what that is. As with free association, thoughts do not necessarily come to your mind quickly. If there is a pause in the thought process, don't worry. An association or image will come.

There are two main differences between free and direct association. One as you just learned, is connecting to a story from a book or movie or song, etc. as opposed to reaching for a personal memory. The second is how in free association you let your thoughts go back and back until they can seem very far away from the dream. Jung keeps direct association close to the dream images or theme. I see it as step out, step back; it's like a dance. Stay close to the dream when looking for a parallel.

Once you have found a similar character or theme ask yourself the following questions. What was the ending to the story? Do you agree with the ending? If not, what do you think would have been more appropriate? Can your new ending somehow apply or suit your current situation? What learning does the story have for your situation?

A Note About Practice and Rehearsal

In describing the example of "becoming" the cat in my dream, I employed a Gestalt rehearsal to help me access my disowned parts. Of course this method is a very behavioral approach to change. I call it "Fake it till you make it," and let me assure you, it works.

But before I leave this section on finding solutions, I want to include another phenomenon from our dreams that is outside our conscious control. In addition to practicing our disowned parts after we wake up, we often find that dreams contain an unconscious rehearsal of the new behaviors we need for solving our problems. These dream "rehearsals" serve a valuable function for our waking lives.

Our dreams provide a safe place to practice new reactions to our current or impending issues until we feel ready to take our new behaviors or emotions out into the world. We see this with Sharon, who knows, her relationship with her boyfriend will soon come to an end. She can unconsciously see it in the way he is pulling away from her. Sharon wakes morning after morning from her dreams with feelings of loneliness, emptiness. Three weeks later, as she unconsciously was anticipating, her boyfriend breaks up with her and Sharon is surprised to discover that she is faring much better than she would have expected. Her lonely dreams were preparatory.

It reminds me of the series of dreams I had in anticipation of going to New York to be on TV, which I mentioned earlier. However different the subject, all my dreams took place in a huge space, in an enormous room with walls far away! By the time I got to New York and walked into the huge television studio I felt surprisingly at ease in my surroundings. My dreams had desensitized me and in the process, relaxed me. If the Gestalt approach is "Fake it till you make it," this aspect of unconscious rehearsal feels more like "Been there, done that." You live the situation or emotion in your dreams over and over again, and by the time the event happens you are ready.

CHAPTER THREE: KAREN'S CIRCLE OF LIFE DREAM

*L*et's look at my sister-in-law Karen's dream. I used this dream in my book in 2002 as an example of connecting yourself to a universal theme or collective image, and couldn't resist drawing upon it again for its simplicity and depth. She amplified a single picture from her dream out to a collective image and universal theme; a simple but deep image.

The dream I am describing came when Karen already knew that her father had cancer and somewhere inside her, that he probably didn't have long to live. This is how Karen herself relayed the story to me. Watch how she amplified the image in her dream right out to a universal image without any extra questions from me.

"Murray and I went for a Christmas vacation to Barbados. Two nights before we were to return to Montreal, I had a dream. The time of year was early spring, when the leaves were still their tiny, tender green. It was a sunny day and my father was wearing a black and white-checked bathrobe and his black slippers. His face was extremely pale. He began to walk in a circle around the tree on our front lawn. As I watched him walk, I noticed that his feet were not touching the ground. When I awoke, I told your brother the dream and expressed my fear that my father was gravely ill and that we had to go home. Seeing that our returning flight was the following day, I decided to wait the twenty-four hours to return. It's funny that I didn't call home. I knew he was sick, and I didn't want to know the answer to my question. Besides, my family did have my co-ordinates.

"We arrived in Montreal at midnight. From the airport, I immediately telephoned my sister. I woke her out of a deep sleep and asked her, 'What's wrong with Daddy?' My sister replied, 'Nothing, Karen. He's fine.' I said, 'Where is Daddy now?' She replied, 'He's at home!' I persisted in my questioning, insisting, 'Where is Daddy?' My sister asked, 'Karen.

Have you had one of your dreams?' I replied, 'Yes.' I was extremely disturbed. I went home with this terribly uncomfortable sensation. I was so certain that something was wrong, and I couldn't relax my body. At four o'clock in the morning the phone rang. It was my mother, who was crying, 'Come quickly. Something's wrong with Daddy!' When I arrived at my parent's house, the paramedics were already there. My father had suffered a massive stroke, which had robbed him of his speech and paralyzed all of his limbs. After six weeks in the hospital, he died."

I stopped to cry. I mean me, Layne.

Karen said, "And you know, it's totally symbolic."

I asked, "In what way?"

She answered, "The tree. Rebirth. The spring. His walking in circles around it. The circle is a symbol of eternity. There is no beginning and no end. The tree was rebirth. My father's feet off the ground, was death. And in the end in fact, his death was a gift to him. It wasn't an old tree. It was a young tree. The color of the tree was that fresh green. I mean, why would I have someone walking around a tree in a circle? And his whiteness; it is such a juxtaposition, having a pale old man walking around the young freshly budded tree. And you know that fresh smell at that time of year? Spring is birth! Winter is the great death and spring is the birth," she said, "especially when you live in this climate!"

As you can see, Karen took great comfort in amplifying the scene in her dream out to a universal level. Jung would have proposed that the image sprang to her spontaneously from the collective unconscious. It was the image she needed to see at that particular time in her life. It is the answer, if you will, to the issue she was facing at the time, the loss of her father. And the comfort the image brings is the knowledge of the never-ending circle of life. A circle is not finite but infinite, continuous, so Karen came away with a sense of hope rather than one of an abrupt ending.

What did she do to get there exactly? It's not like we get to step into Karen's head to know what thought led to the next, but you can see how it went, can't you? She saw the tree, and asked herself what that tree reminded her of. She even spoke as she was remembering, and noticed the fresh green color, the new leaves, and conjured up the smell of spring in her mind. Soon after, she understood the contrast of her father walking in the circle, the old around the new. But the most important piece to see here is that Karen was using her own interpretation from her own understanding of the world. The information resonates so precisely because it all came from her.

Now, while it is optimal for the associations to come from you, that doesn't mean they all have to. That's why I love dreamwork in a group. In *Have A Great Dream, Book 2; A Deeper Discussion: Decoding Your Dreams To Discover Your Full Potential*, I discuss my experience with my Emma-Jo Dream, in which a group member at a conference gave me the very rich, old story of Avalon, King Arthur and Lady Guinevere that I connected to so deeply. A group brings a wealth of ideas to tap into. Just make sure that you feel a strong connection with any suggestions that come from outside. That is the most important part.

This happened with another client, Sophie, whose dream you will read in the upcoming chapter titled Dreams To Practice With. Sophie's Airplane Dream also originated in my earlier book. After hearing her dream, I suggested to Sophie the plot reminds me of the story of Sisyphus. She immediately connected to my idea. Jung would have said that we each connected so firmly to this thought because the motif of frustration as seen in Sisyphus, going up and down but getting nowhere, rose spontaneously from the unconscious. Jung proposed these ideas are ones we already know, deep inside us. We all have a collection of images and characters that we don't need to learn, but are born knowing. The point is that any image, action, or plot in your dream that reminds you of a bigger story can have a special archetypal meaning for you.

A Final Note

Before beginning the chapter of dreams for you to work with, I am going to close with a dream series of my own which I've already referred to, my Kneeling Dreams. I like to use these dreams because they have a wide variety of points of entry and solution-finding techniques. They give a great example of how the deeper you go into the dream the more prizes are waiting for you. It's there for the taking! These dreams demonstrate how much reassurance and help you can get from hooking into the universal element in your dreams.

My Kneeling Dreams

As I mentioned earlier, I had a series of dreams in which I was trying to make my way around on my knees. In one dream, I was clumping around a lower campus of what seemed like a familiar university (maybe Ashville, North Carolina). I was getting around okay until I had to make it up a flight of stairs, which was impossible to do on my knees. There was snow on the ground. I could not stand up. I started to click on the meaning of kneeling only when I shared the dream with my husband. When he heard me say to him, "I couldn't stand up!" he asked me whom I was having trouble standing up to. I swear it was like a knife in the heart! I knew right away he had found the mirror.

A few days later, I dreamed I was on my knees again, this time in the office of a man named Neil. The pun struck me almost immediately! So did the repetition—I was kneeling in Neil's office! When I used a character point of entry searching my associations with Neil, my brother immediately came to my mind. Neil is my brother's age, and has worked with him from time to time. While I wouldn't say he is his close friend, my brother is certainly friendly with Neil. This led me to conclude the dreams were about my difficulty in standing up to my brother. I arrived easily at this conclusion, because I was in fact having difficulty approaching my brother about a certain subject.

The Solutions:

For solution finding I used a character point of entry. Perl's Gestalt technique of becoming a character in the dream revealed that the dream-character Neil was the solution to my problem. Using active imagination, I imagined what Neil's approach would be. The exercise made me realize I had to approach my brother exactly the way Neil would. Besides being friendly with my brother, Neil is a businessman. He represents the part of my personality that speaks to others in a non-emotional, business-like way in order to get my point across. Neil brought out to my conscious mind, once again, the emotional/business-like polarity that I have found often in my experience because my habitual or knee-jerk response is to react emotionally. This response, which sometimes fits a situation perfectly, was not the most appropriate here. In fact, the best way to turn my brother off about an issue is to approach him while being too emotional.

The dream reminded me I had to practice being Neil in this situation. I even borrowed a tie from Andy, and put it on with a vest and jacket of mine when I went to speak with my brother! This kind of approach may feel uncomfortable, but trust me, it can work. You start out mechanical, as if you were in a play, but after a while you become more comfortable. Using the dream's setting, I also decided to speak with my brother in his office, which I knew would help me maintain my business-like, unemotional stance as opposed to his home where it easier for him to remember I am his younger sister.

But there was a deeper level to this dream. I thought to myself, "Why am I on my knees, afraid? Why am I having trouble 'standing up' to my brother?" I wanted to understand whether this dream revealed a pattern in my life. Using Freud's free association, I asked myself where in my past this response originated. The answer came back that I used to behave this way with my father, who was the authority figure in my childhood. So I was transferring my fear of authority from my father (where it rightly belongs, or so I think) to my brother. Now, I felt as though I had re-directed the misplaced fear to the right person.

Looking at my dream from a deeper layer, I learned that it was not only about my relationship with my brother. I had discovered a pattern in my behavior: my habitual response to authority is too emotional. It is both ineffective and inappropriate. Now I was beginning to see that a more "Neil-like" response would be more effective with all kinds of authority.

I was ready to start replacing my old patterns of behavior with this new, business-like approach. My dream revealed a whole new aspect of myself, stronger and more confident.

You might think I was ready to close the book on this dream and start practicing my newfound personality traits by calling my brother right away. But here's where the universal elements in this dream come out into the open. As soon as I started thinking about it, I realized that my issues with authority are actually universal human issues. I asked myself— am I unique in having a fear of authority? Am I the first or only person who has had these feelings? And now we can see that I wasn't alone in my feelings at all. People have always feared authority. So I asked myself, "Who is the ultimate authority figure, anyway?"

I was spontaneously released from my self-judgments as the answer occurred to me— God! God is the ultimate authority. And how many humans through the ages, have stood in fear of God? I immediately connected that people have not stood in fear of God; they have knelt before Him! Kneeling before God is an archetypal image. You find it in culture after culture, through thousands of years. I realized that greater than my fear of authority as represented by my father, is the fear of God.

This helps me direct my fear of my father's authority to a more reasonable place. After all, he was only human. He was not God. In realizing and accepting this, I not only feel less afraid of my father. I am also less angry with him and more forgiving. True, my father made mistakes. He yelled at me sometimes, spanked me a couple of times when I was little, and grounded me as a teenager. This made me feel angry, but now I know that's all right. Once I understand that I responded to my father as if he were a divine authority, I can redirect my fear to God and enter into a fully human relationship with my dad, despite the fact that he is departed.

I still sensed another dimension here though. What exactly am I afraid of? Suddenly I realize—the fear of authority for me is directly linked to a fear of rejection. If God rejects me, He could take away my life, my soul. God might close the Gates of Heaven to me. If my father rejected me, he might have never spoken to me again. These are some of the worst things I can possibly imagine. I have good reason to be afraid.

Let's go back to the dream, though. In the dream I am kneeling, like someone kneeling before God. Maybe I can find some comfort, some strength in my fear by returning again to the universal, archetypal level. So I asked myself who was the first person to kneel before God. The answer came to me right away: Adam and Eve. They were the first couple to worship God. I realized something else, too. Adam and Eve were the first people to be rejected by God! In His wrath God sent His only children out of the Garden of Eden. Probably the worst thing they could imagine actually came to pass. But here's the strength in the story—even after kicking them out of the house, God forgave His children. He loved them. We might not live in Paradise, but we're still around and God still takes care of us. That is what it was like for my dad and me—maybe he yelled at me, or maybe I felt sometimes like he was kicking me out, but I know he always loved me. Even though he's gone now, I still feel the strength of my father's love.

So now I know that my fear of my father ultimately comes from my thinking of him as if he were God. When I remind myself of his humanity, my fear diminishes and so does my resentment. I also remember that there is no danger of rejection, that God will always love me. This makes my fear much less. You know what was the biggest comfort I took from this archetypal image of kneeling? Somewhere inside me, I stopped thinking of myself as such a chicken! When I connected to how every human stands or kneels in fear of someone at some point in his or her life, it brought me together with the rest of the whole world and moved me away from judging myself so harshly. By acknowledging my fear and then accepting myself, I really did strengthen my ability to approach my brother.

In fact, after interpreting my dream I found I was much more comfortable about the whole situation. This happened because once I looked into my dream from a universal level, I moved far away from feeling stuck in my fear about his reactions. My whole perspective widened. I had more confidence because now I understood that my fear didn't actually belong to my brother, but to God. Now, my fear was in its right place.

Something else had changed. My fear of my brother was really a fear of rejection. But now I understand that people can argue, disagree, even yell, without actually rejecting you. What's the worst that can happen in this situation with my brother? He can disagree with me. But if God could banish Adam and Eve from Eden and still love them, if my father could ground me for a week and still love me, surely my brother can disagree with me about an issue without rejecting me. This perspective gave me a much more rational view of the situation, and greatly helped me maintain a "Neil-like" approach.

Of course, like any new perspective on your behavior or your relationships, the wisdom you get from an archetypal understanding of your dreams doesn't soak in all at once. You have to practice. I can tell you though, today I find myself more able to move through my fears in the face of any authority figure, and through any fear of rejection I experience.

So as you can see, while each layer of interpretation of my kneeling dream stands on its own...(excuse the pun), there is great benefit to looking at the universal images in this dream. They have given me the strength to make permanent changes in the way I live my life. I think it is interesting how this dream series shows that as we enter deeper into our own souls, we come closer to the universal human soul. You have seen that the deepest source of my strength in standing up to my brother ultimately arises from the power and faith I feel, just like the Israelites and like many ancient religions, in kneeling before God.

CHAPTER FOUR: DREAMS TO PRACTICE WITH

" ...in the midst of ordinary outer life, one is suddenly caught up in an exciting inner adventure; and because it is unique for each individual, it cannot be copied or stolen."

– M.-L von Franz

From Man and His Symbols, p. 211

Here is a collection of dreams to help you practice the Points of Entry for both decoding the event or problem you are discussing with yourself, and finding solutions in your dreams. The Dream Maps for each example appear at the end of the dream discussion.

To help you understand and practice what your own choices would be, at the end of each dream I will prompt you to explore different points of entry. I would like you to think about the points of entry you would use, before you read my analysis. Don't be shy! Dreams have many points of entry and while they sometimes each take you to a different learning they all get you somewhere good!

Allow me to explain the process a little of analyzing someone else´s dream. First I need to say that countertransference is absolutely unavoidable when doing dream analysis. What is countertransference? Countertransference is present whenever the analyst brings her own experiences to your dream. Inevitably, her emotions from her own past and life will colour her response to you. It involves a therapist unconsciously and mistakenly prioritising his emotions and needs over yours.

In the section titled Decoding and Mapping the Dream, I described how our associations to people, places and things are as unique to each of us as our fingerprint. You have your own unique database, or, for those of us over 50, a filing cabinet for your associations to the dream symbols.

I say that countertransference is unavoidable because your unconscious mind has inside it every single memory and association you have ever had since you were born. You can ask five different people to think about horses and all five may love them, but they still will not share exactly the same feelings and associations about horses. Take me for example. I love horses and used to ride as a child, until one day, my saddle wasn't strapped on tightly enough and started slipping slowly to the side until I was practically riding off the horse's side at a 90 degree angle! So while I do still love horses, my unique association about "starting out feeling secure, and then losing that feeling," is mine and mine alone. So for that matter is the fact that I never did get back on a horse after that experience. If I am working with a person who dreams about a horse, my own associations are going to be there. Unavoidable.

A cure for this dilemma was developed by Dr. Montague (Monte) Ullman, who used his knowledge of neurology and psychiatry to understand the brain function of dreaming. Dr. Ullman developed an experiential dream group process, which he clearly detailed in his book, Appreciating Dreams from 1996. Dr. Ullman emphasized that only a procedure which follows precisely every stage as described in his book should be called Ullman's Dream Group Process. With my utmost respect for his work, the concept I present here is inspired by Ullman's work. I believe it offers a sure-fire way to keep your finger on countertransference when listening to someone else's dream.

In order to maintain complete respect for the dreamer's use of symbols and metaphor, when offering the dreamer ideas you think may be present in his or her dream, you should begin your sentences with "If this was my dream….."

So if my niece, who has won many awards for her riding, had a horse in her dream, I would respectfully offer, "If this was my dream, I would be looking for some situation in my current life in which I used to feel secure but I'm no longer feeling that way." Further, I'd be wondering if it is a person or situation I may have loved, but that I am preparing to leave.

There's no "This is what your dream is about," or, "This is the reason you had this dream," or "The horse in your dream means strength, power, endurance, virility and sexual prowess." Those dictionary-style interpretations don't work. You won't find my niece's associations to competition, success, and a host of other personal connections and feelings in a dream dictionary. Neither will you find anything about security versus insecurity for me.

You cannot "tell" anyone what their dream is about. You can tell them what it might mean if you had a dream like theirs. This concept is very rich when you experience it in an actual group. Because we share so many human experiences, the projections the dreamer hears from the people sitting in the circle saying "If this was my dream.....", are precisely what might help him "click" on why he had his dream!

In closing this subject, I am compelled to add that the experience of using "If this was my dream. . ." gives you an incredible opportunity to exercise that muscle we so often let atrophy. I'm talking about the empathy that respects the feelings of other people instead of assuming you know how they feel. You don't. Too often, not only do we imagine we know exactly what someone else is thinking or feeling, but we respond to what we think someone is experiencing, without even asking the person. Without even considering that we do not have mindreading powers! Dream analysis gives you an opportunity to practice asking a person to share their experience instead of telling them what their experience is.

So as I said, at the end of each of these practice dreams but before you read my conversation with the dreamer, please think about what points of entry you would use and what questions you might ask the dreamer if you were the interviewer. Take out a sheet of paper and write them down. What if you were the dreamer? How would you answer?

Here to remind you is the list of points of entry you can use for both decoding the dreams and for solution-finding.

Decoding the Dream: Points of Entry

1. Isolate the Feelings
2. Identify the Symbols, Metaphors, or Characters
3. Play on Words and Puns
4. The Action
5. The Plot
6. Repetition

Solution-Finding: Points of Entry

1. Direct Solution
2. Take the Dream Story Outside to Waking Life
3. The Action
4. Jung's Active Imagination
5. Symbols, Metaphors and Characters; (A Gestalt Approach)
6. Polarities
7. Self-Regulation
8. Looking Back in The Mirror
9. Finding Your Archetypes

Jodie's Renovation Dream

I thought we were still renovating the bathroom because there were bits of construction material lying around on the floor, but when I went in to take a bath, I noticed that the side panel and base of the bathtub had been pulled off. It was sort of just dangling there barely attached to anything.

Giving a puzzled look to my boyfriend Michel, I said, "What the heck did you do?" I was wondering how he expected me to bathe in this unstable thing that can't hold water. He didn't respond. I pulled and flipped it on the ground and only then did I realize that he had installed the new bathtub behind it. To my surprise, he'd done the installation properly without asking me a million questions.

The new tub was a standard white. The old one that was now lying flat (with one end slightly curled upward like a toboggan) was sort of an embossed copper, like those metal tiles people sometimes use on their kitchen walls. I pushed it with my foot through another door to a big, empty hall.

It was a really thin sheet. The downward side was slippery and I jumped on it and started skateboarding around the dining room. It was so much fun. I was surprised at myself that I was able to do it. I'm usually scared of skates and boards because I think I can't balance myself. I have no control over what they do. But I was shifting my weight and gliding around in circles, stopping when I wanted. I felt proud. I was having a great time until my parents walked in through another door.

They asked me what I was doing and I answered, "skating." The rest of our conversation no longer came out in words. It was some kind of telepathic communication where all at the same time, I could hear them thinking, "Isn't that dangerous?" and "Why are you doing that?" My thoughts answered, "No. What's dangerous about that?" and "Because it's fun and I can do it!" With that, I went back to skating.

Now it's your turn. Let's see what point of entry would you use? What part of the dream grabs your attention? What aspect might you ask Jodie a question about? Will you want to start with the symbols and ask about the tub? Will your questions be about Jodie's feelings? Have fun with whatever point of entry you like and see how it fits with what actually happened for Jodie.

My Discussion and Analysis with The Dreamer:

Jodie is living for a year in Asia as part of her university studies. She has been away from home for six months. Since her boyfriend Michel appears in the dream I wanted to test if the dream is actually about him or if Jodie used her boyfriend as a metaphor for someone else.

"Is your boyfriend with you in Asia?"

"No, but he was here visiting for the holidays a month ago."

"Is there in fact construction going on at your house back in Montreal?"

"There is always some construction going on at our place! My boyfriend demolishes rooms and then rebuilds them."

As you can see, I am checking the facts from the dream with the facts from Jodie's waking life. Since she says she is surprised in the dream that he had done the installation properly without asking her a million questions, I asked if he typically does seek her advice when working.

"Yes." she responded. "He gets me involved all the time, because he has trouble making decisions." She added, "I feel so frustrated when he comes at me with a million questions. I have no expertise whatsoever in construction!"

Using the plot as a point of entry, I have taken a mental note that Jodie's boyfriend's behavior in the dream is not what she would typically expect.

Now I focused on the symbols. "Tell me about the tub."

"The front of the old tub which I thought was unstable was really only a façade. It was a decorative, thin, copper sheet, with a square mosaic design as I described earlier that you would find in someone's kitchen. It is concealing the 'standard white' tub."

She added, "The standard white tub is utilitarian as opposed to the more artistic but less functional old one I can see."

I see a shade of a repeat here, and point it out to Jodie. "There's a similarity in you expecting your boyfriend to behave a certain way (asking many questions) and in the dream he doesn't, and thinking you are looking at an unstable old decorative tub, but really behind it is a sturdy, standard white one. If it was my dream, I would be thinking about if there is a recent situation in my waking life in which things are not as they appear to be or anyway as I thought they are."

A third image, once decoded, points to the same thing. While Jodie says she is usually scared of skates and boards because she feels she can't balance on them, there she is skateboarding in the dream, even gliding around in circles. This leads me to ask, "Is there some situation recently where you thought a situation or expected a person to react one way, and turned out to be another?"

Hearing my question Jodie is thinking, but doesn't "click" on anything specific.

So I moved on to other repeating imagery I had noticed. In the dream, Jodie asks her boyfriend, "What the heck did you do?" and later in the dream her parents are asking her telepathically, "Why are you doing that?"

This repeat spurred my question, "Is there any situation where you may be wondering why someone is doing something? More importantly they are doing something they don't normally do? Is anyone behaving differently than what you would typically expect?" Here is what Jodie offered.

"My friend Iris has started working a second job. I worry about her new job because she is working with someone who is all business. She's doing it to make money. She says she's okay, but I'm not convinced."

Going with the character, I asked Jodie to describe Iris. She said, "She's like me, drawn to the artistic side. That's why I worry about her being happy in a business-like environment. But at least she will be making money and it does seem to be okay. It is certainly better than her current day job, which she hates!"

Noticing the mirror I remarked, "Your description of your friend and her circumstance has the same ring as your description of the bath tubs. One more artistic, less stable, the other more traditional, utilitarian."

While the story about Jodie's friend Iris "fits" as a possible mirror, it still wasn't a big "Aha!" for Jodie. Typically when you hit on the meaning of your dream it resonates so well inside you. I can hear it in the voice and see it on the face of the dreamer, and so far I'm not seeing that.

Jodie said, "You know while we've been talking, something else occurred to me. I was working as a mentor at the university in Montreal last year. A little while ago, I discovered the girl I mentored posted on her Facebook page that she is thinking about traveling to Singapore and hoping anyone who has lived here or knows someone who does, might answer some questions for her to help her decide if she should come to Asia or not.

"I corresponded with her and answered all her questions. Her questions make me ask myself what my experience is like here. I don't like it so much, but it's such a challenge it is actually creating a new confidence in me. I am relying on myself, and what I can do! I think the experience is important. It makes me believe in my abilities more and more.

"I received an email from this student so fast. Even too fast. She wrote something like, 'Thanks. Based on the information you gave me I'm going to go ahead and submit the application.'

"I feel so responsible! It reminds me about when I first came here six months ago. I remember when I first got here asking myself, 'What am I doing here?'"

Jodie hearing her own question aloud echo the dream, shifted into a click about its meaning for her. It made me ask, "What did you decide was the answer to the question?"

Jodie said, "I decided I would spend the year focusing on myself. It's going to be about me. I'm the style of person who is always feeling responsible for others. I made a promise to myself I am going to spend this year here in Singapore taking care of myself."

"Have you been successful so far focusing on that goal?"

Jodie admitted, "Well, up until these last few weeks, yes. I have been taking care of myself. But a few events have been making me worried about maintaining that balance. Receiving the email from the student I mentored, saying she made such a quick decision based on my responses to her questions, triggered me feeling responsible again. Then there is my friend Iris who I worry about. To top it off, my boyfriend's cat died recently. He isn't the type of person who easily expresses what he's going through to friends, and he shares his feelings with me. I need to be there for him. Finally, there are the people I've met here in Singapore. One person I know is feeling sad, I am affected by it, and have been slipping back to feeling responsible for people in general. As you can see, it's everywhere!"

So it is Jodie herself who has been responding differently than she expected! We now understood the repeating plots and images. The funny part which really made it come together was her expression about how she was "slipping back" into old patterns. What a great example of play on words! In the dream Jodie says the downward side of the copper sheet was slippery. The part of the "old" tub or the "old" way of responding was slippery. We had found the dream.

Solutions:

The language Jodie uses when recounting her dream reveals one of several solutions. For example, the way she says, "I'm usually scared of skates and boards because I think I can't balance myself. I have no control over what they do. But I was shifting my weight and gliding around in circles, stopping when I wanted. I felt proud."

This is terrific! While the metaphors help Jodie express her feelings of responsibility and lack of control when friends and family are experiencing problems, the action in the dream shows her shifting her weight and stopping when she wants! She is maneuvering herself. The dream provides a rehearsal for the action Jodie needs to take.

This is a perfect example of what I was explaining earlier about our habitual responses. We tend to respond with the same knee-jerk, over-invested reaction without regard for the uniqueness of each relationship and situation. Jody's dream shows her an image of her ability to respond individually. She can shift her weight and take different positions deciding how much, if any, involvement she wants to have in any given situation. In separating our knee-jerk reactions from other potential we have, we start by looking at each life situation on its own. For example, how close is Jodie to the person feeling sad? Does she feel the same level of responsibility to a person she's known for a few months as she does to her boyfriend who lives with her?

The most important thing Jodie says when describing her dream is, "I can stop when I want." True. Jodie realized that the ability to stop when she wants is the solution her dream offers. She is typically fearful of skating and boards because she thinks she "can't balance" on them. Isolating each situation will help her create a balance. Of course change is scary, especially when considering how others will react to our change in behavior. We see by the action in the dream that Jodie moves past her usual fear and goes skateboarding.

I love another thing that Jodie said when describing her fear of skating or boarding. It was that she feels she "has no control over what they do." What a terrific and accurate comment! We have no control over what others do. We don't control how they respond to their own life crises and we also have no control over their reactions to the changes we decide to take for ourselves!

The Plot or Story Using Free Association

Hoping for some free association to the feelings the dream brings up, I asked, "Where do you think the idea of you feeling responsible for people in your life comes from?" Jodie shared, "I have a younger brother who I have always felt responsible for."

I offered, "It's so normal to expect the elder sibling to adopt that role." Jodie responded, "I used to live with my grandparents when I was a kid and all the older cousins lived there too. In fact I used to look after them even though they were older!"

I am focused on the sturdy tub that lies concealed behind the old unstable thing that Jodie described, "…can't hold water." Using a Gestalt framework I explained, "Jodie. You are the tub. You are both the artistic side, which you show to the world, but underneath, as you describe yourself, is a sturdy, white, dependable, utilitarian tub. That's the side that holds water. It's the part of you that knows how to take care of business. It's the opposite of unstable."

The dream reminds Jodie about her interior strength. This will help her "tap" into that strength. There's another pun. Get it? Bath? Tap? I know that might sound funny to you, but the images and how they tie together in a dream I never consider random.

You will remember that tapping our memories from the past lets us pose the question, "Do I as an adult agree with how I was treated back then? Is this the same response I would have with my own children?" Using memory as a point of entry I asked, "Jodie, how old were you when you lived with your older cousins at your grandparent's home? Do you think it was a good idea that you were made to feel responsible for your cousins? Was it appropriate? Were they a lot older than you?"

"From the age of three to nine my cousins lived with us. One of them was a few months older than I was and the other two were both two years older than me. My bother was born when I was ten, so from eleven on I was responsible for him.

"I didn't mind at the time with the older cousins, but I did resent having to look after my brother because it was a different kind of responsibility. I took on the cousins' welfare out of my own sense of fairness, but in the case of my brother it was imposed on me.

"In response to your question, I don't think it was appropriate for the adults to have created a situation where I felt I needed to protect my cousins, but I think I've been putting other people's needs above my own since then because I'm doing some kind of penance for having been the privileged one."

As I pointed out earlier, becoming aware of your habitual responses doesn't make them disappear. Of course not. It's what you are most accustomed to. Once you have done this exercise, you will start to recognize your initial reaction to situations and I assure you, after you understand where your reactions are coming from, you will start to catch yourself when you respond this way. After a while, someone like Jodie will find it easier to say, "Oh, here I am feeling responsible again." Except now she'll be adding, "Wait a minute. Am I really responsible for the decision my friend Iris makes concerning her job? Do I have any control over her decisions? Do I even want any control over her life decisions?"

I pointed out to Jodie, "Instead of responding in autopilot the same way you would have back then with your cousins and brother, now when thinking about the student you mentored, for example, you might catch yourself realizing with awareness that you are not nine years old anymore, and she is not one of your cousins or your brother. This is not a situation in which you need to feel "more privileged" or in which you feel you need to repent.

"Once we have an awareness of origin, we automatically begin having the ability to separate situations. This result is almost unavoidable, especially in view of the fact that you don't think it was appropriate that you were somehow put in the position of feeling responsible for others at such a young age. I know you aren't nine or eleven anymore but nothing stops you from metaphorically taking your freedom; your childhood back."

Jodie is already there. We can see it in the dream. It is her parents' "voice" she hears in the dream. It's the voice we all have inside us that started way back when. I like how she says it was telepathic. It's a voice we hear in our head saying "Isn't that dangerous?" and "Why are you doing that?" all at the same time.

I offered, "In the dream, your thoughts answered, 'No! What's dangerous about that?' and 'Because it's fun, and I can do it!' You say you went back to skating. You are rehearsing. We can see you have already begun the process of letting go of the old voices. You are individuating! Taking back your sleeping parts. The dream is a picture of all that. Soon you will find it easier to "slip" into your new responses. In other words, you can go on and get into that sturdy safe tub!" Using Jung's Active Imagination, I reminded Jodie she can go ahead and get in the tub! There's only room for one in there and that'll help her focus on herself and her own needs. While she's at it she can enjoy a good soak!

Jodie's Renovation Dream

I thought we were still renovating the bathroom because there were bits of construction material lying around on the floor, but when I went in to take a bath, I noticed that the side panel and base of the bathtub had been pulled off. It was sort of just dangling there barely attached to anything.

TROUBLE MAKING DECISIONS

MYSELF WHEN I ARRIVED IN ASIA
①

Giving a puzzled look to my boyfriend Michel, I said, "What the heck did you do?" I was wondering how he expected me to bathe in this unstable thing that can't hold water. He didn't respond. I pulled and flipped it on the ground and only then did I realize that he had installed the new bathtub behind it. To my surprise, he'd done the installation properly without asking me a million questions.

SURPRISED
×2

WHITE, UTILITARIAN, TRADITIONAL

DECORATIVE ARTISTIC (IRIS) CONCEALS NEW TUB

The new tub was a standard white. The old one that was now lying flat (with one end slightly curled upward like a toboggan) was sort of an embossed copper, like those metal tiles people sometimes use on their kitchen walls. I pushed it with my foot through another door to a big, empty hall.

SURPRISED
③
FUN

It was a really thin sheet. The downward side was slippery and I jumped on it and started skateboarding around the dining room. It was so much fun. I was surprised at myself that I was able

68

to do it. I'm usually scared of skates and boards because I think I can't balance myself. I have no control over what they do. But I was shifting my weight and gliding around in circles, stopping when I wanted. I felt proud. I was having a great time until my parents walked in through another door.

PROUD

SOLUTION

They asked me what I was doing and I answered, "skating." The rest of our conversation no longer came out in words. It was some kind of telepathic communication where all at the same time, I could hear them thinking, "Isn't that dangerous?" and "Why are you doing that?" My thoughts answered, "No. What's dangerous about that?" and "Because it's fun and I can do it!" With that, I went back to skating.

2

2X REPEAT= DOING SOMETHING I DIDN'T THINK I COULD DO
= MOVING TO ASIA / SKATING

3X SURPRISED

Sophie's Airplane Dream

I was in the cockpit of a two-seater airplane. I was sitting in the co-pilot's seat, but I had no controls in front of me. The pilot had all the controls. It could have been a large commercial plane because he had many stripes on his arm, but it was not, because I could tell by the controls it was a small plane. Each time we flew up to a certain altitude, the sun was there shining in our faces. Though we put both visors down, mine did not block out the sun's brilliance. Each time we rose to a certain altitude, the plane would have engine trouble, go putt, putt, putt, and we would have to go back down, and get another plane. It was not as though it was ever an emergency, panic, or scary situation. It was only engine trouble. I never saw more than the pilot's arm. It was the most frustrating situation!

Sophie added, "My dad has all those stripes. He was a pilot, and a military man too."

I asked, "Is your dad the person you would depend upon to help you?"

"Well, if any person could get me there, it would be him, but even the pilot in the dream could not!"

It's your turn again! Don't read ahead to my discussion with the dreamer until you try this exercise! If you were sitting with Sophie after hearing her dream, what would your first point of entry be? For example, if you choose a symbols point of entry, what questions would you ask? How about the action in the dream? Are there any other points of entry that you notice with this dream?

My Discussion and Analysis with The Dreamer:

"Are you currently experiencing frustrations in your life?

"Yes! There are two issues in my life that frustrate me to no end. First is that my grandmother died a few months ago. Just the thought of me never being able to see her again knocked me for a loop. Besides that, since she died, my mother and I have been in constant conflict. Add to that frustration that I have been in court with a messy divorce, which also causes me tremendous frustration. My ex-husband hasn't paid any child support on the false grounds that he was unable to afford the costs. After years in court, when I had finally proven his fraud and won the case, he skipped the country. We don't even know where he is."

Looking for a wider view of the past, I inquired, "In the dream the pilot would seem to fly up successfully, but as you describe, is forced to come down to earth again. What comes to your mind about stripes on a pilot's sleeve?"

"The amount of stripes a person has is an indication of their authority, or leadership."

"Was your father an authority figure in your childhood?"

"No," she responded emphatically. "While I am and always have been so close to my dad, it's my mother who was and continues to be the authority figure in our house. My father had absolutely no control over her."

I offered, "So in his waking life, your dad has lots of stripes and authority, but in the dream he's flying a tiny plane that he can't keep up in the air."

"Exactly. The size of the plane doesn't fit the stripes. You know in the last few days, I've been thinking maybe he would step in and say something to my mother on my behalf. "

"It sounds like you are saying you were hoping for him to take all the control of the situation. That's the picture of your dream. You say you are a co-pilot, yet you have no controls in front of you.

"What comes to your mind about the plane, or for that matter about planes in general?"

"Planes get you where you need to go. The big, commercial ones are powerful. The two-seater plane in the dream is powerful enough to get us off the ground but has weak staying power."

The small size of the plane illustrates the reality of Sophie's situation. She was not feeling big and powerful in her life.

Solutions:

Listening to Sophie describe her dream, I felt struck by the plot and the action of the story; they go up in the air and each time they get to a certain altitude, the plane can't make it and they have to come back down. The event keeps repeating itself again and again. It was that continuous up and down movement that hooked me. I saw these two people, going up and down and up and down, and never going forward.

As I explained earlier using the story or plot from a Jungian perspective, you would ask yourself, "Is there any story that I have ever heard that has a similar ring to it? Where else have I heard this?" The process I am talking about is the same as comparing Shakespeare's Romeo and Juliet to West Side Story. There you see two separate stories written so many years apart from each other, and yet the main plot is the same.

In the up and down frustration of Sophie's dream, I saw the story of Sisyphus. Sisyphus, a Greek mortal, was punished by the gods who made him roll a huge rock up a hill for eternity: whenever he reached the top, the rock would roll back down, and he would have to start all over again. Now doesn't this seem like what happened to Sophie in her dream? By the way, please feel free to disagree with me as we go through these hypotheses (which after all, is all they are). I invite you to see what story you might think of and discover what learning is waiting inside it. But for now, since Sophie connected to the story of Sisyphus, let's examine what Sophie might take from it.

There are two aspects of the story that offer strength and learning. The first is the most obvious: Sophie's frustration is universal. It is part of the human condition when we realize we cannot see someone who has died. The story of Sisyphus tells us that it is pointless to push against the way of God, the way of life. Sophie, like the rest of us, has as little chance of escaping the reality of loss as Sisyphus did in going against the gods. So I imagine Sophie can direct this story to the loss of her grandmother. At least she is not alone in her suffering, and maybe her surrender is the first step to acceptance.

The second lesson from the story of Sisyphus comes from asking, "How is this character behaving? Do I have something to learn from his behavior? Can I find some strength in reacting like he does? Do I want to act like him in my current situation, or is the story there to show me how I don't want to react?" Look at Sisyphus. Let's be honest. He's as doomed as Romeo and Juliet were. He has no control over his situation. He is doomed for eternity, powerless over his fate. What about Sophie? Does she want to be like this guy? Would you want to be like this guy?

I realize Sophie feels like Sisyphus. I even understand how that imagery, as Jung would have said, spontaneously rose up from her unconscious because in fact she is behaving as if she has no choice or power to change her situation. But is she really powerless? No actually, she isn't! While Sophie's efforts at winning control over her ex-husband or her mother's behavior are doomed for eternity, she can choose not to be like Sisyphus! How? By understanding the element of her life that she does have the power to change, herself. She can change her own attitude.

The myth of Sisyphus illustrates the positive and negative power of the archetypes. In the conclusion to Man and His Symbols, M.-L. von Franz wrote, "...we can see that the archetypes can act as creative or destructive forces in our mind: creative when they inspire new ideas, destructive when these same ideas stiffen into conscious prejudices that inhibit further discoveries" (Jung, 1969, p. 304).

Sophie was stiffening and inhibited, stuck in her "I am powerless" mode like Sisyphus. Yet if you find an image like that in your dream, you can use it to search out ways to take your power back! Taking control and rising up strong in the face of adversity and great frustration is also a universal, timeless, human characteristic. This is the positive potential we can draw from the image of Sisyphus.

We can't control the behavior of someone else. Sophie felt great disappointment and frustration while growing up from her father's inability to stand up to her mother. But the example of Sisyphus might help her start the process of respecting her father's experience in his relationship with her mother as separate from her own. This might even encourage Sophie to accept her situation with her ex-husband and move on.

As you have already learned in this book, we have the ability to change our imagery, to change our minds. With Jung's active imagination as my tool, I explained to Sophie, "The solution to this dream is for you to move over to the pilot's seat! Take control! Although there are issues in life (like death), which you do not have control over, there are so many events, which are in your control. This dream is about getting in touch with the aspects of your life you can take control of. It is about letting go of depending on someone else to lift you up!" Unlike Sisyphus, Sophie did have ways to escape from her pattern. She needed to find a job in order to care for her children, something her ex-husband clearly would not do. And what about her situation with her mother? Sophie is not doomed for all eternity while her father fails to resolve her conflicts. Sophie has the power to approach her mother on her own.

So let's look again at how Sophie and I connected the themes or pictures in her dream to a universal human dimension. In Sophie's dream it was the movement that caught my attention, that motion of going all the way up, getting nothing for the effort, and coming down again, over and over. This, along with the feeling of frustration, led me to Sisyphus. First we saw a theme or a movement in the dream. Then we looked for another similar theme from another story. Sophie's dream told a story about doing the same thing again and again but getting nowhere. Then, once we found another story we looked for the lesson in it. This is how to employ Jungian solution finding.

My Decoding Point of Entry: The Feelings, The Action
My Solution Point of Entry: Jung's Active Imagination and The Plot or Story Using Jung

Sophie's Airplane Dream

I was in the cockpit of a two-seater airplane. -GETS YOU WHERE YOU NEED TO GO
-POWERFUL BUT WEAK STAYING POWER

I was sitting in the co-pilot's seat, but I had no controls in front of me.
MY DAD ——→ DEPEND ON HIM FOR HELP
The pilot had all the controls.
AUTHORITY + LEADERSHIP

It could have been a large commercial plane because he had many stripes on his arm, but it

was not, because I could tell by the controls it was a small plane. DAD=SMALL CONTROL
MOM WAS "AUTHORITY",
NOT DAD

Each time we flew up to a certain altitude, the sun was there shining in our faces.

UNSUCCESSFUL
Though we put both visors down, mine did not block out the sun's brilliance.   EFFORT

FRUSTRATION! Each time we rose to a certain altitude, the plane would have engine trouble, go putt, putt, putt,

and we would have to go back down, and get another plane.

It was not as though it was ever an emergency, panic, or scary situation.

It was only engine trouble. I never saw more than the pilot's arm.

It was the most frustrating situation! ⎯ GRANDMOTHER'S DEATH
⎯ MESSY DIVORCE

Sophie added, "My dad has all those stripes. He was a pilot, and a military man too."

I asked, "Is your dad the person you would depend upon to help you?"

"Well, if any person could get me there, it would be him, but even the pilot in the dream could

not!"

76

Danny's Giraffe Dream and Map

I woke up this morning with this dream. I was watching a CNN news report alerting the public that a giraffe had escaped from the local zoo. The story featured a computer-generated giraffe moving rather than a film.

There was a map of Chicago in the background. Other people were in the room. I don't know them.

In the next scene I was at my mother's house. I got up and walked into the washroom. When I opened the door, to my amazement right there in the bathtub as big as life itself was the missing giraffe! I was shocked and in a complete panic.

Not wanting to alarm the giraffe, I backed away slowly and closed the door. I immediately headed to the kitchen to call 911. I told them my name and gave my address, explaining I have the giraffe.

In the next scene, I was sitting at my mom's kitchen table with the anchor from CNN. She had piles of books around her and was looking up something in one book and then going to another. She's heavy set, wearing a track suit, and not very attractive looking.

Suddenly the bathroom door opened and my wife's cousin walked out, saying, "Hi you guys! How are you?"

Here we are again! It's your turn. What points of entry would you use if you were decoding Danny's dream? For example, if you choose the giraffe as a symbol, what questions would you ask him? How about the feelings Danny experiences in the dream? Are there any other points of entry that you notice with this dream?

My Discussion and Analysis With The Dreamer:

The giraffe is the focal point of this dream. But what did it symbolize in the dreamer's life? And how was the giraffe dream a mirror of his current situation? We started by focusing on Danny's emotions during the dream. I asked him, "How did you feel when you were watching the report on TV?"

"I thought it was interesting, especially them showing a computer-generated giraffe."

"And how did you feel when you saw that giraffe right there in front of you?"

"I was shocked, and filled with a mixture of awe, excitement, panic and amazement," he said.

I asked, "What do you think might be happening in your life that's very big? Are you filled with awe, amazement and maybe some panic about anything? Are you feeling you have to be cautious about something?"

"Not really. I don't feel panicked about anything. I'm not so connected to caution either."

Since we are not always in touch with our feelings, I moved on to the symbols. "Tell me what a map is. Imagine I have never seen one."

"A map is drawings of places. It shows you where the places are and how to get there."

"Okay. What about giraffes? What comes to your mind when you think about a giraffe?"

"They have very long necks. It reminds me how exciting it is to see one. I remember being a child and being filled with awe seeing them. They are SO big!"

"Come now, Danny. SO big? There must be something going on in your life that is out of the ordinary. Take a guess."

Taking your first guess on the situation your dream is addressing is always a great idea. Your first guess usually works because that's what you had on your mind, consciously or unconsciously, while you were awake before the dream!

And with that, he caught his dream. "Well my wife and I are expecting our first baby. As a matter of fact she had an ultrasound yesterday." We connected the computer-generated giraffe to the ultra-sound image of his child that he had just seen the day before. Danny's dream captured well the mixture of emotions he was experiencing in anticipating the new arrival that would suddenly appear right in his home, like the giraffe in the tub.

Now that Danny connected his dream to a waking life event, we continued. I admit I am always looking for a confirmation that the dreamer has hit on the correct mirror. I typically find what satisfies me by looking at other "matches." Once you click on the subject of the dream the other pieces start to fall into place.

Danny's associations to his mom are that she is a caring, concerned person who is loving and helpful. Nine-one-one he described as a place where you can call for help, and CNN is news. He associated the tracksuit to his wife, whom he said had recently taken to wearing them all the time. He also shared she had been reading about the first, second, and third trimesters in all these different books she'd been buying. Just like the reporter!

I was convinced he caught the dream after that link, not to mention the family member connected to his wife (just like the baby) who suddenly "appears from nowhere as if she belongs."

Finally, it seems as though the giraffe transforms from the water in the tub (a metaphor for his wife's womb) into a family member and arrives as miraculously as his wife's cousin suddenly walking right out of the bathroom!

The Solution:

By now I am confident we are on the right subject, and am looking for possible solutions to Danny's apprehension. The dream offered Danny a way to deal with his anxiety. Looking at the action point of entry, what did he do when he saw the giraffe in the dream? Danny immediately went to the phone to dial for help. That is precisely what Danny was not doing in his waking life situation. In fact he was gripped by panic at the thought of his new arrival, but did not express his feelings to anyone.

Danny's dream pointed him toward the response that was missing in his waking life situation, and showed him that he could take a new approach to dealing with his anxiety: he could ask for help. Danny and his wife are not alone. The dream takes place in his mother's kitchen, one person he can reach out to for help and advice whenever he needs it.

Remember how I said symbols often having multiple meanings? Having gotten the hang of it, Danny called me the next day to tell me how fascinating a choice his unconscious had made in using a giraffe. Not only did the giraffe capture the hugeness of the coming event and his own feelings of awe, but the long neck bears a connection to the cervix. This shows exactly how the dream symbols fall into miraculous place!

Finally, let's look at the full map, which includes the dream's repetition. If I had never met the dreamer and I looked at the repeats, I could already make some guesses. I would ask the dreamer to keep family members in mind since he referred to family three times in the dream. Then I would ask if he has a situation in his life that brings him a sense of awe. Finally, the dream decoded reveals different people and ways to obtain help. Four ways one can reach out for help and knowledge. Beautiful.

> **My Decoding Point of Entry:** The Feelings and The Symbol
> **My Solution Point of Entry:** The Action

AWE X2
FAMILY MEMBER X3
HELP X4

LONG NECK
AWE = EXCITEMENT
SO BIG!

AWE = 2

Danny's Giraffe Dream

INTERESTED {

I was watching a CNN news report alerting the public that a giraffe had escaped from the local zoo. The story featured a computer-generated giraffe moving rather than a film.

SHOWS YOU WHERE PLACES ARE + HOW TO GET THERE

HELP = 1

There was a map of Chicago in the background. Other people were in the room. I don't know who.

CARING, CONCERNED
LOVING, HELPFUL

HELP = 2

SHOCKED-
AMAZED
AWE +
PANIC

AWE = 1

In the next scene I was at my mother's house. I got up and walked into the washroom. When I opened the door, to my amazement right there in the bathtub as big as life itself was the missing giraffe! I was shocked and in a complete panic.

FAMILY MEMBER = 1

CAUTIOUS {

Not wanting to alarm the giraffe, I backed away slowly and closed the door. I immediately headed to the kitchen to call 911. I told them my name and gave my address, explaining I have the giraffe.

HELP = 3

COMPLETE
SURPRISE
HOW SHE
APPEARS
FROM
NOWHERE
AS IF SHE
BELONGS

In the next scene, I was sitting at my mom's kitchen table with the anchor from CNN. She had piles of books around her and was looking up something in one book and then going to another. She's heavy set, wearing a track suit, and not very attractive looking.

NEWS

HELP = 4

FAMILY

Suddenly the bathroom door opened and my wife's cousin walked out, saying, "Hi you guys! How are you?"

FAMILY MEMBER = 2

FAMILY MEMBER = 3

81

Sue's Poo Dream

I am in a resort. I am my own age. I have a little girl with me who has blond hair. She's two years old. In reality I have a grown son, not a daughter.

The resort is very busy. There are so many people there. We're in the pool and the little girl tells me she has to go potty. After we got out of the pool my mother was suddenly with me.

We were in this giant room filled with people. My mother was across the room from me squatting like a Chinese person would and looking at me. The little girl is next to me, and poo appears all over the place!

I hadn't even taken her diaper down yet and I started to put it into my mouth. It isn't the shape of regular poo. It's the same color as chocolate milk. I put it in my mouth and started to clean it and spit it out.

When I'd spit the poo out it was like little white blocks. It sort of looked like cheese. So it went into my mouth like a chocolaty color and it came out white.

I kept doing that and my mother said, "What are you doing? Why are you doing that? Are you crazy?" I just looked at her. I didn't respond.

I wasn't grossed out in the dream. It seemed normal. After a little while I took the little girl's diaper down. She wasn't dressed in swimming clothes. In fact she had leggings on. As I took down her diaper all of the feces came pouring out, but now it looked almost like diarrhea."

With all this poo appearing in Sue's dream, I would love to be in the room with you to hear what your first point of entry would be. Will it be the poo? Or maybe it will be the plot and how the color and shape change to little white blocks! What are your questions in your conversation with Sue? Are there any other points of entry that you notice with this dream?

My Discussion and Analysis With The Dreamer:

Of course I always have my pen ready to map a dream, but after hearing Sue's dream I put the map on hold for the point of entry that was screaming at me.

I explained, "There are certain people in my life who when I want to say something to them, I have to think about how I am going to say it keeping in mind I still have to say what I have to say. I might have a dream like yours at a time like that, especially if I have some shit to say to somebody and it's building up inside me, but I have to be careful about how it comes out. You put the shit in your mouth and you clean it up before you spit it out. Does that resonate with you at all? Is there someone in your life who you have something to say to this week that you are considering how to come out with it? It could be your mom, but not necessarily. I only name her because she appears in your dream, but you may have chosen your mom to represent someone else. If it really is your mom, she would be a great example of someone who we often have to clean things up before we come out with it. I don't mean clean in the literal sense. I am saying it metaphorically. Saying something with caution and care around it instead of in a harsh or blatant way."

After a knowing 'Aha!' Sue shared, "Well, you know the day I had this dream I was shopping with my mother. There were a lot of abusive things that were said to me as a child especially by my mom and I've been spending some time with her wanting to talk about this and let it go, but you know, she doesn't get it. You know how people will say things to you but they don't even remember they said it? Well things stick with me forever. My mother wonders why I remember everything and wishes I would just let things go. She doesn't appreciate I am trying to resolve the past precisely so that I can let it go!" Sue closed with saying, "When I went to sleep last night I was praying I could let go of what she was saying to me."

Using a character in the dream, I explained to Sue the little girl is a part of her own self. Sue wondered, "Why do you think the little girl is blonde and as a child I was dark haired?" I responded, "Yes! Of course the little girl is different than you. In the dream, she's the one letting it out. Literally. And you are the one taking what comes out of her and stuffing it back in. Literally. If this was my dream, the act of my pulling her diaper and her tights down would be me pulling away all the barriers I have used to hold my feelings in all these years. My feelings even turned into diarrhea. For me that represents something I can no longer hold in."

Further, I explained, "Using the little girl in the dream captures how the story stretches all the way back to when it started for you. Of course before we let something go, we first have to let it out! It seems like that's what you are doing in the dream. It's a great metaphor. With poo, we can only hold it in for so long until it has to come out."

I added, "You don't have to express these feelings to your mom necessarily in order to accomplish this end. You can share your feelings with a friend or family member you trust. The important point is you are taking care of your little girl; the little girl inside you. You are feeding her your adult voice now, as opposed to the voices you were brought up with. The little girl looks different than you because she is different from you!"

Solutions:

This dream points to at least two items for discussion. First, Sue says her mom is a person who will never take responsibility for her behavior in the past. When you are dealing with a person like that you aren't going to get anywhere by simply holding your ground, insisting she was abusive. This won't make it better. In my work with dreamers I often say the bottom line is finding a way to get what you need.

Once you know what you need, you can ask, is the behavior in the dream appropriate to the situation? In this case, as Sue discovered, she needs to find some way to communicate her feelings to her mom.

One possible solution from the dream comes from the metaphor about Sue "cleaning up" what she wants to say before it comes out of her mouth. If this is her decision, the dream affords her a rehearsal for editing how she speaks to her mom about her feelings. Alternatively, Sue might decide to share her uncensored feelings with a friend or trusted family member.

Additionally, this dream offers the following lesson: it is never too late for us to begin caring for our inner child. As this dream shows, Sue has already begun doing that.

Final note: I am not surprised the dream takes place in a resort, with the play on words in this discussion about what approach Sue will "resort" to in order to let go of her past.

My Decoding Point of Entry: The Action
My Solution Point of Entry: The Action

Sue's Poo Dream

I am in a resort. I am my own age. I have a little girl with me who has blond hair. She's two

years old. In reality I have a grown son, not a daughter.

The resort is very busy. There are so many people there.

We're in the pool and the little girl tells me she has to go potty.

After we got out of the pool my mother was suddenly with me. WAS ABUSIVE TO ME AS A CHILD
I WAS SHOPPING WITH HER
YESTERDAY

We were in this giant room filled with people.

My mother was across the room squatting like a Chinese person would and looking at me.

The little girl is next to me, and poo appears all over the place!

I hadn't even taken her diaper down yet and I started to put it into my mouth.

It isn't the shape of regular poo. It's the same color as chocolate milk.

I put it in my mouth and started to clean it and spit it out.

When I'd spit the poo out it was like little white blocks. It sort of looked like cheese.

So it went into my mouth like a chocolaty color and it came out white. 1. CLEANING UP WHAT
YOU WANT TO SAY?
2. IS THAT 'NORMAL' ?

I kept doing that and my mother said, "What are you doing? Why are you doing that?

Are you crazy?" I just looked at her. I didn't respond.

I wasn't grossed out in the dream. It seemed normal.

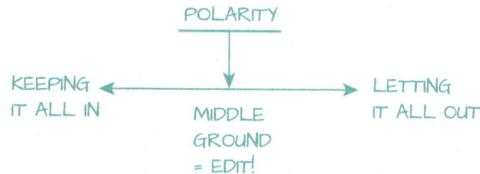

SEEMED
NORMAL

After a little while I took the little girl's diaper down.

She wasn't dressed in swimming clothes. In fact she had leggings on.

As I took down her diaper all of the feces came pouring out, but now it looked almost like

diarrhea." SOMETHING YOU
CAN'T HOLD IN

POLARITY

KEEPING   ←——————————→   LETTING
IT ALL IN   IT ALL OUT
                        MIDDLE
                        GROUND
                        = EDIT!

Ethel's Homeless Dreams

I have been having dreams for about a month that I am homeless. It's never exactly the same. Some examples are how in one dream I'm living under a bridge. In another I'm living in my car and in a third dream I'm living in an abandoned building, but I am always homeless.

I'm not doing anything in the dreams. I don't seem to be upset. I'm just sitting there accepting my fate! When I wake up I'm upset, but in the dream I have resigned myself to the fact that I am homeless.

If you were sitting with Ethel, what part of this dream sticks out at you? Is it her feelings you would want to inquire about? Is it the setting or mood in the dream? It's all up to you. Take the opportunity to compare your inclinations with how my conversation with Ethel went, and remember! Any point of entry you choose is a good one!

My Discussion and Analysis With The Dreamer:

I inquired, "Is there a current situation that you are resigning yourself to?"

Ethel said, "Yes. There is. I live alone. My daughter lives out of state. I've just resigned myself to the fact that I am going to be alone and I'm okay with that."

Since Ethel seems to be "resigned" in all the different places the dreams occur, I asked, "I know you are always homeless in the dreams but it looks like you are trying it out in different places. Are you? For example, if these were my dreams I'd be focused on the fact that I seem to be going to several different places while I am in the state I'm in. It's an alone state." To this I added, "Do you actually do a lot of different things? Do you go to clubs? Are you involved in social things?"

Ethel said, "No. I am not involved in anything. I am not a very social person."

Solution and Strength:

Here is a perfect example of how dreams give us the opportunity to stretch ourselves. Even though Ethel's habitual behavior is not socializing, the dreams give her the idea to check about different activities and groups she might become involved with.

Realizing the dreams' rehearsal quality, Ethel can take steps to emulate the plot in the dreams. For example, she needs to move to find art classes, dance, bridge classes or whatever suits her fancy, and get herself out to different places, same as she's doing in her dreams. Even though Ethel will still be alone in her living situation, she need not be alone in her days.

The fact that Ethel says she has resigned herself to being alone is, in itself, the act of letting go. This is a very positive aspect and strength in the dreams. Even if she hasn't completely resigned herself, the dreams are setting the stage for Ethel to accept her solitude and do something about it.

My Decoding Point of Entry: The Feelings, Repeating Image and The Plot
My Solution Point of Entry: The Action

Harriet's Brother-in-law Dream

I dreamed my brother-in-law was murdered. Mike Tyson was the murderer.

It's funny, because my brother-in-law really did just telephone me yesterday.

It's also funny because yesterday was also the day after Mike Tyson had bitten someone's ear off.

I almost didn't answer the phone when he called. I was busy.

In the dream I felt so relieved that I had spoken to him.

Imagine if I hadn't picked up the phone? And then he died?

I would have felt so guilty!

In the dream, my sister-in-law had to tell his mother the sad news.

It's your turn now! Are you getting the hang of it? I think it so important to go with what calls you or what aspect of the dream attracts you first. Is it the movement Harriet employed in answering the phone in her waking life? Using a symbols point of entry, is it Mike Tyson you would question Harriet about? Whatever point of entry you use and questions you decide you would ask Harriet, once you are done, read on and see if you and I chose the same route to get there!

My Discussion and Analysis With The Dreamer:

"How did you feel in the dream?"

"I felt complete panic at the news."

"Did your feelings change at all during the dream?"

"Well, once it occurred to me I had answered the phone when he called the day before, I felt a sense of relief."

"Tell me about your brother-in-law. What kind of personality is he?"

"He is sensitive, loving, and caring." Then she added, "He is also extremely organized and efficient."

"What about your sister-in-law?"

"She's more loose and relaxed than he is. My sister-in-law is easy-going and carefree. For example, she keeps her house so messy and seems fine about it!"

Already, we see three polarities present themselves. One is of "panic" versus "relief," another is "orderly" versus "messy." A third is the male and female couple.

"Can you connect any situation in your life recently in which you are feeling a sense of panic mixed with relief?"

"Well, yes. My husband has decided to move us from our home here in Maine to downtown Seattle, Washington! On the one hand, I feel relieved to move back to city life. I often feel bored here. Then again, I feel the panic setting in because, like my sister-in-law, my house is in a state of complete disorganization. I feel panicked because the move is coming up very quickly."

The Solution:

In a metaphoric way we could say that the ability-to-be-organized part of Harriet's personality was murdered. When mapping a dream, here is how I illustrate polarities:

Brother-in-law _____ Sister-in-law
organized/efficient _____ disorganized/messy
complete panic _____ easy going/carefree (relief)

Have you ever heard the statement that all anxiety is future-oriented? I love that principle. It is true for sure that anxiety happens in our head. It's something we conjure up with thought. In this case, Harriet's anxiety comes from contemplating her move, which in fact isn't happening at this actual moment. It's going to happen, but not yet. Action on the other hand, means making a physical movement right now. Harriett can start organizing and packing right away. The truth is when you are in motion there's not much time for anxiety. The movement gets not only your body in motion, but it focuses your thoughts on what you are doing in the moment.

Harriet was sitting still in her state of panic and disorganization. A dream's goal in presenting polarities is typically to help us move off the extreme behavior we are holding on to and towards the middle of the spectrum.

Looking at the action or movement in the dream, Harriet took care of business when she answered the phone, even though she was distracted. Her having taken "action" had her feeling relieved. There's the solution right there. Harriet needed to become more like her brother-in-law. Adopting her brother-in-law's style of organizing her house for the move would serve two purposes: to become so busy she had little time to panic, and to get ready for the move!

In Bruce Lee: Artist of Life, Lee talks about the curative power of awareness, saying, "Now, if we are willing to stay in the center of our world and not have the center either in our computer or somewhere else, but really in the center, then we are ambidextrous. Then we see the two poles of every event. We see that light cannot exist without non-light. If there is sameness, you can't be aware anymore. If there is always light, you don't experience light anymore. You have to have the rhythm of light and darkness. Right doesn't exist without left" (Bruce Lee, 2001, as cited in Farnam Street blog).

My Decoding Point of Entry: The Feelings
My Solution Point of Entry: Polarities, Characters

Harriet's Brother-in-law Dream

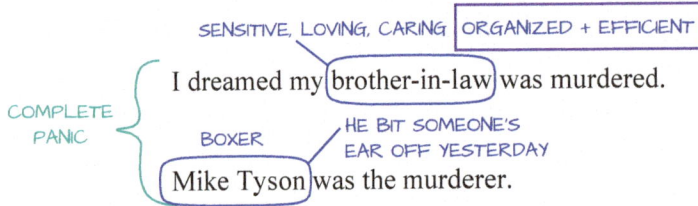

SENSITIVE, LOVING, CARING | ORGANIZED + EFFICIENT |

COMPLETE PANIC

I dreamed my | brother-in-law | was murdered.

BOXER   HE BIT SOMEONE'S
         EAR OFF YESTERDAY

(Mike Tyson) was the murderer.

It's funny.

RELIEF

He really *did* just telephone me yesterday.

Actually, I almost didn't answer the phone when he called.

I was busy.

TAKE CARE
OF BUSINESS
=RELIEF
=SOLUTION

In the dream I felt so relieved that | I had spoken to him. |

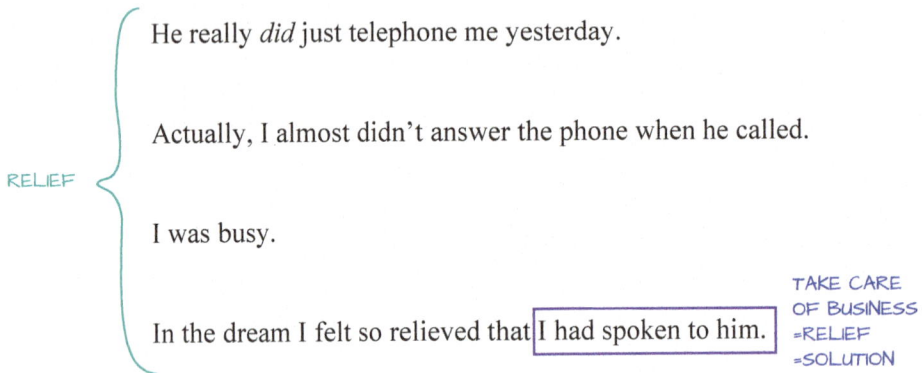

Imagine if I hadn't picked up the phone? And then he *died*?

I would have felt so guilty!

LOOSE, RELAXED,
EASY-GOING, CAREFREE

My | sister-in-law | had to call and tell his mother the sad news.

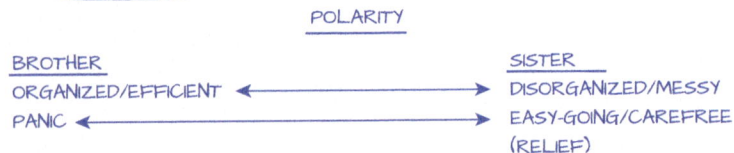

POLARITY

BROTHER
ORGANIZED/EFFICIENT ←————————→ DISORGANIZED/MESSY
PANIC ←————————→ EASY-GOING/CAREFREE
                                  (RELIEF)

SISTER

92

Gloria's Dinghy at the Falls Dream

I'm aboard a very large rubber dinghy. We'll be taking a tour.

The chef on board comes forward on deck preparing something for the dish he will be serving us later. The raft-like craft is tethered not to move away from shore. It has an upper wheelhouse. Not everyone is aboard yet.

The captain is waiting to take tickets and show people aboard.

When I go to the front, the bow/prow and look over, I see the dinghy is stationed right at the edge of a tremendous waterfall! It reminds me of Niagara Falls.

There are various boats lined up across the falls, all right at its edge too.

I am wondering, "Is this to be a race? It will surely be thrilling! It will be a once-in-a-lifetime adventure, for sure!"

Spray from the falls rises up, spewing from below obscuring the fall's real depth, and then the dinghy slides silently off the precipice.

I expect a rough, tumbling ride, but instead it's almost like we're floating down and out through the mist in slow motion. I am thinking to myself, "How curious, riding in space."

We enter the mist and nothing else matters.

Here's your chance to try out some points of entry that work for you. Remember you don't even have to imagine it's Gloria's dream you read. Go ahead and imagine it was your own dream! What questions might you ask yourself? Is it an action point of entry in the water falling over the falls? Or perhaps you want to ask yourself about the dinghy?

The Pre-Analysis

Two weeks before the Dinghy at the Falls Dream, Gloria had two other dreams, which once analyzed, reflected a recent experience she had with her daughter at a family affair. The main themes and repeating plot in the previous two dreams were images and action relating to expectation versus experience. The earlier dreams also repeated the idea of instability, especially in the face of her expectation versus her experience. Instability, for example, appeared in an image where Gloria was trying to maneuver herself on loose planks of plywood with no banister to hold.

These earlier dreams were reflecting Gloria's visit to a family affair and her expectation of seeing her daughter, who had moved to a distant continent. Gloria was looking forward to catching up after not having seen her for almost a year, but this expectation turned out to be a big disappointment. She travelled early in anticipation of having time to connect with her daughter, but her daughter never met with her. The experience turned into another case of Gloria stuck inside her habitual response, where she imagines and hopes for closeness despite the fact that her relationship with her daughter is an ongoing, unstable dynamic that in any of her previous efforts, has so far, never changed.

We are working things through in our dreams. It is a process, and if you catch a few dreams over a period of weeks, like Gloria did here, you can actually see the progress. The Dinghy at the Falls Dream tells the whole story and then illustrates where Gloria is now. Finally, during the "pre-analysis", Gloria also shared that the day before the Dinghy Dream, she had telephone conversations with both her brother and her son.

My Discussion and Analysis With The Dreamer:

"How did you feel in the dream?"

"I felt excitement at first to be there, but then I was shocked and fearful when I saw the dinghy was at the edge of the falls. I'm afraid of heights.

"Once the dingy actually dropped over the falls with me, though, I felt amazement! I am not in control of what was happening. It is slow and surreal, but it's just happening, and it's okay.

"How curious it was riding in space, entering the mist and nothing else matters.

"Finally, at the bottom I felt safe. I knew all is well."

I offered, "From what you are describing it sounds like all the events of the last few weeks are played out in this one dream. You described your excitement at the thought of seeing your daughter, at the family affair and even travelling there early to see her. Then your shock at how your feelings and expectations were not reciprocated."

While discussing the two earlier dreams, Gloria had decided to stretch herself in future and manage her unrealistic expectations. The idea of rising to new "heights" of behavior towards her daughter gave her some fearfulness. Change is never easy. It is our natural human inclination to feel discomfort and so resist change, even at the potential risk of detriment to ourselves.

I continued, "What an apt description of what transition feels like! You know that feeling when you finally take the jump into something, not knowing how it's all going to turn out?

"Just looking at this description you can see there has been a shift from your experience with instability in the dreams you had a few short weeks ago.

"If this was my dream it would be the visual of me letting go. Letting go of the fantasy that I have any control over how my daughter behaves. The dream is a picture of me letting the change happen. The change is in my expectations, and my dream is an illustration of me embarking on new attitudes for approaching my daughter in the future."

Listen. It's hard enough to change oneself, never mind trying to change someone else. Now that's a situation in which we truly are powerless.

"What comes to your mind when you think of a dinghy? Describe it for me."

"A dinghy is a rubber boat, usually on board a ship that they use for people to go ashore on. The ship and the dinghy are water vessels that are together, but they separate and function independently of each other."

"And what would you say a chef is?"

"A chef is a cook who gives you good food, and food gives you sustenance."

The Solutions:

Looking at the plot in the dream, I pointed out, "Although it seems as if you don't have control in this dream, the truth is you are not just with the dinghy. You are the dinghy! As you say, the dinghy functions independently."

Gloria responded, "It's easier for me to see this change that is happening as out of my control than seeing myself as being the fearless dinghy. After all, if I adopt a somewhat cooler, distanced attitude towards my daughter, she might see me as uncaring. Well, maybe it's me who might see myself as being uncaring!"

I offered, "I like the definition you gave about the dinghy. It's a great example of how the unconscious sometimes uses the same metaphor for several reasons. In your description of the dinghy, we can see it as your daughter having separated from you, (the mother ship). Though from your description of the current situation, it appears that now she's the ship and it's you who, is now the dinghy separating from her! At the beginning of the dream, you even have yourself 'tethered' to her! You going over the falls, is a jump over to your new behavior or attitude."

Being a mother myself, I can appreciate Gloria's discomfort in adopting an approach more in line with her daughter's behavior towards her. As she accepts herself as the dinghy, Gloria will have progressed that much farther on her path towards change, or maybe this process has already begun.

Thinking about her dream, Gloria said, "I love how I felt in the end. I'm going with the ride and whatever happens, happens."

Earlier in this book I described Adler and his theory about how dreams prod us forward, giving rise to an emotion we can run with. That's Gloria, in her own words, "going with the ride."

I have also discussed how our thoughts and lives, both inside and outside our dreams, form one fluid reality. They all come together in the same thought process. That's why I accept all aspects of my discussion with the dreamer, whether inside or outside the dream, as part of the same whole.

With this principle in mind, when Gloria described her telephone conversations with her brother and son the day before the dream I did not downplay their importance. These family members, both of whom are very close to her, are included in her thought process concerning her daughter.

Gloria doesn't go over the falls by herself. There are other people on the boat with her. In fact this gave Gloria the clue to one of the solutions from her dream.

"My daughter is not going to give me what I need and want. The good news is that I can get it from other family members. My son's girlfriend for example, treats me as if she is my natural daughter."

"I certainly. Agree! Tell me, what are your associations to Niagara Falls?"

"The top of the falls with its horseshoe shape is what stands out for me. It's the first thing that comes to mind about the falls."

This reminded both of us of one of Gloria's dreams from two weeks previous, which took place in a blacksmith's house that Gloria was redecorating.

When our dreams reveal a progression on an issue over a period of weeks, I call them reevaluation dreams. Let me explain. You know when you break a leg and a few weeks pass, you might look back and see how you have come along? You might think, "Wow. A few weeks ago I was in the hospital and now I may be shaky but I am up and walking." Our dreams show us how we are moving along on an issue.

We accomplish this function in our dreams by choosing the same image once decoded. In Gloria's case she used a horseshoe. Both her Blacksmith's House Dream from two weeks before and her Dinghy at the Falls Dream contained this image. The horseshoe reminds Gloria of her dad, who used to fit their horses on the farm with shoes.

Now, Gloria is using the image of a horseshoe again but relating to it quite differently than before when she was "redecorating" (changing) in an "unstable" atmosphere. Get it? Horses? Stable?

Reminded of her dad she shared, "If I wanted to do something he disapproved of he used to say, 'It's your choice but you have to live with the consequences.'"

She added, "My father was a liberal. He gave us the opportunity to think for ourselves. So we thought about things a little longer knowing we wouldn't be punished as much as we would punish ourselves. We learned from our own mistakes."

What lesson from Gloria's past can she apply to her present situation with her daughter? Gloria realizes she agrees with her dad's approach. By reminding herself to follow her own instinct and take responsibility for her choice, she found the courage to forge on and over the falls so to speak.

An old hand at dream analysis like myself, Gloria could not leave this dream without digging just a little deeper and so off we went to Jung.

I prompted, "Choose an image from the dream and sit back for a bit. Tell me what story or TV show or poem comes to your mind when you think about that image."

"I would choose the Falls and what it felt like being up there. It reminds me of Jack and the Beanstalk. He tried to reach something, climbing up and up high. So high up. I have a fear of heights. He's so high up in the clouds, and I'm so high on the Falls. I can't see the bottom below for the mist and neither can Jack."

I was watching Gloria, asking myself what this story has to teach us. I said, "Do you remember what happened to Jack? He went up there to steal the chicken that lays golden eggs. And do you remember how he was saved from the giant chasing him?"

"Yes!" she offered. "He had to cut the vine! I have to cut the vine."

It seems like Gloria is well on her way to forging a new approach to her relationship. In my opinion, the stalk supplies a wonderful visual metaphor for an umbilical cord!

It's a funny thing about changing our roles in families and with friends. Even though we have no control over changing anyone but ourselves, the fact is when you make a change, those around you change too. It's like removing a piece from an infant's mobile. At first everything is off balance and shaking. But after a bit each piece rebalances in a new stable position.

I remember in her book The Two-Step: The Dance Towards Intimacy, Eileen McCann, using some of the work by Virgina Satir, teaches us about how the thorny path of love is nothing less than a highly choreographed dance that steps around issues of power, distance, and intimacy (Satir, 1983). I am not surprised that the solution to Gloria's Niagara Falls Dream reminds me of The Two-Step book. Isn't it true that if you move forward towards someone in a dance, they will automatically move back? And once they start to move forward it is you who is moving back!

As for me, my money's on Gloria. As soon as she starts backing up and cuts her expectations away, her daughter will start moving towards her.

Gloria's Afterthought

A week or so after we analyzed Gloria's dream, two thoughts occurred to her. First, in recalling her Blacksmith's House Dream, she described, "There was one heck of a lot of 'firewood' piled up everywhere to feed the fire! Yet there was only a wood stove for furniture in the large open room. It makes perfect sense to me, that this relates to my relationship with my daughter, at least my expectations for warmth and how they can't be met. I have plenty of warmth to stoke a fire, but in the case of my relationship with her, no place to burn the wood."

Here's the second. "In August, the time before December when I last saw my daughter, I had the expectation of spending some 'quality' time with her too, but when my husband and I flew to Vermont where she was staying, instead of spending the day with us, she and her boyfriend flew off to Niagara Falls for the day!"

Isn't the unconscious mind miraculous with its ability to weave hidden connections? This explains one of the reasons why, after 45 years, I remain so passionate about dream analysis.

My Decoding Point of Entry: Feelings, Repeating images (Niagara, horseshoes)
My Solution Point of Entry: Symbols, Rehearsal, The Plot using Freud, and The Plot using Jung

Gloria's Dinghy at the Falls Dream

COOK GIVES FOOD
= SUSTENANCE

RUBBER BOAT →
SHIP SEPARATES
TO TAKE PEOPLE
ASHORE. FUNCITONS
INDEPENDETLY OF
EACH OTHER

EXCITED

I'm aboard a very large rubber dinghy. We'll be taking a tour.

The chef on board comes forward on deck preparing something for the dish he

will be serving us later.

The raft-like craft is tethered not to move away from shore.

It has an upper wheelhouse. Not everyone is aboard yet.

The captain is waiting to take tickets and show people aboard.

SHOCKED
+
FEARFUL

When I go to the front, the bow/prow and look over, I see the dinghy is

stationed right at the edge of a tremendous waterfall!

HORSESHOE SHAPE= DAD
-MAKE A DECISION + LIVE
WITH CONSEQUENCES
-LEARN FROM YOUR
MISTAKES

It reminds me of Niagara Falls.

There are various boats lined up across the falls, all right at its edge too.

AMAZEMENT
-NOT IN
CONTROL
BUT SAFE

I am wondering, "Is this to be a race? It will surely be thrilling!

It will be a once-in-a-lifetime adventure, for sure!"

Spray from the falls rises up, spewing from below obscuring the fall's real depth,

and then the dinghy slides silently off the precipice.

I expect a rough, tumbling ride, but instead it's almost like we're floating down

and out through the mist in slow motion.

PEOPLE (NOT ALONE)
'EG.' 'SON'S GIRLFRIEND'

I am thinking to myself, "How curious, riding in space."

We enter the mist and nothing else matters.

I'M GOING WITH THE RIDE.
WHATEVER HAPPENS,
HAPPENS

Finally, at the bottom I felt safe. I knew all is well.

CONCLUSION

I want to offer one final, crucial benefit to understanding our dreams: With the self-examination and self-change that accompany dreamwork, we move our attention away from trying to change others. Think about it. For every minute we spend looking in for what we can change about ourselves, we have spent the exact same amount of time *not* looking out at trying to change someone else.

Given that we are powerless in the business of changing someone else, this is great news. Our time is surely better spent working through and growing from our own self; the only place we can have success in change!

In the introduction to Carl Jung's book Man And His Symbols, John Freeman relates the story of how Jung was asked to write a book on dreams for the general public and initially refused, only to change his mind in the aftermath of a dream. In the dream, Jung saw himself delivering a lecture in a crowded square. The enthusiastic response of the dream-crowd persuaded him to write his book. He claimed he consulted not only his conscious mind, but also his unconscious.

This story defines the essence of my never-ending enthusiasm for dreamwork. Like the Jungians, I believe that the ability to understand our dreams provides us with the opportunity to be completely in touch with our whole selves when making decisions. Interpreting our dreams is not only fun and interesting, it is important.

If you take the time to understand your own dreams, they will show you where you have been, where you are now, and where you are going in your life. They will show the whole of you. Your dreams can reveal the two points that color your opinion whenever you take a position towards any situation: who you are in the framework of your past, and what stage of life you are in at present. Your dreams help you place your current life issues in these contexts. Then you can move ahead, using the power that this knowledge gives you.

For me the feeling of moving through life without a sense of who I really am, besides being boring, would be like driving my car in a strange country without a map. I hope you will make use of the tools in this book to draw your own map! As we've seen over and over, analyzing our dreams can help us use this map of ourselves to increase the efficacy of our actions and improve our relationships. And as I've witnessed in my own life and other people's, the path of self-knowledge can lead us not only toward better decisions but also to peace within ourselves, and forgiveness for others.

ABOUT THE AUTHOR

- 1988 - Certificate in Gestalt Counseling
- 1992 - Studied dreamwork at the Alfred Adler Institute
- 1995 – Present: Member of the C. G. Jung Society
- 1997 – Present: Founded The Dream Interpretation Center, Montreal
- 1997 - Present: Member of The International Association for the Study of Dreams
- 2005 – 2009 Board of Directors, International Association for the Study of Dreams
- 2005 – Present: Lecturer at Concordia University, Montreal
- 2021 – Present: Oprah Daily (oprahdaily.com) Dream Catcher Column -
- 2020 – Present: Psychology Today - Understanding Dreams Column -

Layne Dalfen's interest in dreams stems from her experience in Freudian analysis 50 years ago, where dreamwork was the primary tool. In 1988 she became a Gestalt Counselor, and later went on to study dreamwork at the Alfred Adler Institute. Layne founded The Dream Interpretation Center in Montreal in 1997 and in the same year became a member of The International Association for the Study of Dreams, where she sat on the Board of Directors. She has taught dream analysis to the counseling students at Concordia University in Montreal, since 2005.

Besides having been a guest on hundreds of radio and podcast shows across The U.S. and Canada, Layne enjoys her appearances on Canada's nation-wide Breakfast Television, and Coast To Coast AM, where people call in and talk with her to find the meaning of their dreams. She is a frequent speaker at spas, including Rancho La Puerta Spa in Mexico.

Layne writes a regular column for Psychology Today, titled Understanding Dreams, and is also very well-known at Oprahdaily.com, where they call Layne their "in house" Dream Catcher, the name of her column.

While she continues to do private consultations, Dalfen also offers speaking engagements for companies, tailored to teach teamwork, problem-solving, creativity, and fun which she calls a Dreaminar®. Dreaminars® and workshops for those wishing to learn Layne's unique system are also available for schools, and keynote events.

During these lectures, as well as in her books *Have A Great Dream, Book 1; The Overview,* and its companion work titled *Have A Great Dream, Book 2; A Deeper Discussion: Decoding Your Dreams To Discover Your Full Potential,* Layne's goal is to introduce the general public to the value of understanding their dreams. She provides the tools needed to decode your dreams which makes both short and long term change available to us all

ENDNOTES

In the section titled Theories of Dream Interpretation

1. Here is how Freud himself described free association. "...The patient should take up a....." (Freud, 1938, p. 192).

Reference:
Freud, Sigmund, The Interpretation Of Dreams p.192.

2. "If I now consult my own experience with regard to the origin of the elements appearing in the...."

Reference:
Freud, Sigmund, The Interpretation Of Dreams p.239.

3. Jung wrote, "I call it 'collective' because, unlike the personal unconscious, it is not made up of individual and

Reference:
Jung, C. G. Memories, Dreams, Reflections Glossary, p.p. 401 & 402 The Structure and Dynamics of the Psyche, CW 8, By C.G. Jung pp.133 f.

4. It was Jung who first suggested that dreams can compensate for these distortions in the way we see things, slanted by the overinvested parts of our character (Jung, 1969, p. 62).

Reference:
Jung, Carl G., Man and His Symbols. p. 62

5. As Perls suggests, "You see how you can use everything in a dream. If you are pursued by an ogre in a dream, and you become the ogre, the nightmare disappears. You re-own the energy that is invested in the demon. Then the power " (Perls, 1992, p. 190).

Reference:
Perls, Frederick S., Gestalt Therapy Verbatim, p. 190

6. "You do not allow yourself—or you are not allowed to be totally yourself. So your ego boundary shrinks more and more. Your power, your energy, becomes " (Perls, 1992, p. 31).

Reference:
Perls, Frederick S., Gestalt Therapy Verbatim, p. 31

In the piece on Sophie's Airplane Dream:
In the conclusion to Man And His Symbols, M.-L. von Franz wrote, "…we can see that the archetypes can act as creative or destructive forces in our mind: creative when they inspire new ideas, destructive when these same ideas stiffen into conscious prejudices that inhibit further discoveries" (Jung, 1969, p. 304)

Reference:
von Franz, M.-L. Man and His Symbols Conclusion: "Science and the unconscious." p.304
In the section titled Dreams To Practice With
1. "…in the midst of ordinary outer life, one is suddenly caught up in an exciting inner adventure; and because it is unique for each individual, it cannot be copied or stolen."
 M.-L von Franz
From Man and His Symbols, p. 211

Reference:
von Franz, M.-L. Man and His Symbols. Part 3. The Process of Individuation, p. 211

2. In Harriet's Brother-in-law Dream I wrote:
"Now, if we are willing to stay in the center of our world and not have the center either in our computer or somewhere else, but really in the center, then we are ambidextrous. Then we see the two poles of every event. We see that light cannot exist without non-light. If there is sameness, you can't be aware anymore. If there is always light, you don't experience light anymore. You have to have the rhythm of light and darkness" (Bruce Lee, 2001, as cited in Farnam Street blog).

Reference: Bruce Lee: Artist of Life

Lee, B. (2001). Artist of Life. North Clarendon, VT: Tuttle Publishing. As cited in Bruce Lee on Self Regulation versus External Regulation (2015, January 2). Retrieved from https://www.farnamstreetblog.com/2015/01/bruce-lee-self-regulation-versus-external-regulation/ 3. From Gloria's Dingy at the Falls Dream I cite one of Satir's methods, but it is not a quote. Satir, V., & Baldwin M. (1983). Satir Step by Step: A Guide to Creating Change in Families. Palo Alto, CA: Science and Behavior Books.

SUGGESTED READING

In this book I have not had time other than to give you a quick overview of the different schools and methods of dream analysis. For those of you who wish to learn more, these are some of the best sources of dream interpretation that I have covered in this and my more in depth book of the same name, along with other non-dream books related to my discussions therein.

Adlerian Dream Interpretation

Adler, A. (1956). The Individual Psychology of Alfred Adler. New York, NY: Basic Books.

Gold, L. (1988). A Contemporary View of Dream Interpretation and Therapy. [Festschrift, Pfeiffer 1988

Gold, L. (1978). Life Style and Dreams. In Baruth & D. Eckstein (Eds.), Life-style: Theory, practice, and research. Dubuque, IA: Kendall/Hunt.

Children's Dreams

Siegal, A., & Bulkeley, K. (1998). Dreamcatching. Every Parent's Guide To Exploring And Understanding Children's Dreams And Nightmares. New York, NY: Three Rivers Press.

Dream Dictionaries

Crisp, T. (1994). Dream Dictionary. (Wing Books, distributed by Random House Value Publishing Inc., N.J., 1994)

Fontana, D. (1994). The Secret Language of Dreams. London, UK: Duncan Baird Publishers.

Todeschi, K. (1995). The Encyclopedia of Symbolism. New York, NY: Berkley Publishing Group.

Dream Interpretation During Illness

Garfield, P. (1992). The Healing Power of Dreams. New York, NY: Simon & Schuster.

Freudian Dream Interpretation

Hall, C. S. (1954). A Primer of Freudian Psychology. New York, NY: The World Publishing Company.

Freud, S. (1938). The Interpretation of Dreams by Sigmund Freud. In A.A. Brill (Ed. and Trans.), The Basic Writings of Sigmund Freud. New York, NY: Random House.

Freud, S. (1973). An Outline of Psycho-Analysis. London, UK: Hogarth Press. Translation by James Strachey

Mitchell, S. A., & Black, M. J. (1995). Freud and Beyond: A History of Modern Psychoanalytic Thought. New York, NY: Basic Books.

Thomas, D.M. (1981). The White Hotel. London, UK: Cassell Group/Indigo.

General Dream Interpretation

Bulkeley, K. (2000). Transforming Dreams: Learning Spiritual Lessons from the Dreams You Never Forget. New York, NY: John Wiley & Sons.

Delaney, G. (1997). In Your Dreams. New York, NY: Harper Collins.

Faraday, A. (1980). Dream Power. New York, NY: Berkley Publishing Group.

Fromm, E. (1980). The Forgotten Language. New York, NY: Random House.

Sheppard, L. (1994). Wake Up to your Dreams: A practical self-help guide to interpretation. London, UK: Blandford Press.

Taylor, J. (1993). Where People Fly and Water Runs Uphill: Using Dreams to Tap the Wisdom of the Unconscious. New York, NY: Warner Books.

Van de Castle, R. (1994). Our Dreaming Mind. New York, NY: Ballantine Books.

Gestalt Dream Interpretation

Polster, E., & Polster, M. (1974). Gestalt Therapy Integrated, Contours of Theory & Practice. New York, NY: Random House/Vintage.

Perls, F. S. (1992). Gestalt Therapy Verbatim. The Center for Gestalt Development [Gestalt Development Center in Harrisburgh, PA?]

Stevens, J. O. (1973). Awareness: exploring experimenting experiencing. New York, NY: Bantam Books,.

Jungian Dream Interpretation

Bly, R., & Woodman, M. (1998). The Maiden King: The Reunion of Masculine and Feminine. New York, NY: Henry Holt and Company.

Bosnak, R. (1988). A Little Course in Dreams. New York, NY: Random House.

Bosnak, R. (1996). Tracks In The Wilderness of Dreaming. New York, NY: Dell Publishing.

Hall, J. A. (1983). Jungian Dream Interpretation: A Handbook of Theory and Practice. Toronto, ON: Inner City Books.

Jung, C. G. (1969). Man and His Symbols. New York, NY: Doubleday. First edition by Ferguson Publishing (1964)

Jung, C. G. (1989). Memories, Dreams, Reflections. (R. Winston & C. Winston, Trans.). Recorded and Edited by Aniela Jaffé, (New York: Random House, 1963; Vintage Books edition 1989). From the Glossary: Commentary to Secret of the Golden Flower, CW 13, The Collected Works of C.G. Jung, par. 31, mod and also Civilization in Transition, CW 10, The Collected Works of C.G. Jung, par.803

Sharp, Daryl. (1998). Jungian Psychology Unplugged. Toronto, ON: (Inner City Books.

Woodman, M. (1982). Addiction to Perfection. Toronto, ON: Inner City Books.

Psychic and Precognitive Dream Interpretation

Bro, H. H. (1988). Edgar Cayce on Dreams. New York, NY: Warner Books.

Magallon, L. L. (1997). Mutual Dreaming. New York, NY: Pocket Books.

Ryback, D. (1988). Dreams That Come True. New York, NY: Doubleday.

Sexual Dreams

Delaney, G. Sensual Dreaming How To Understand and Interpret the Erotic Content of Your Dreams. Ballantine Books, 1995 (Formerly titled Sexual dreams.) (A Fawcett Columbine Book, Ballantine Books, a division of Random House Inc., New York, 1994)

Hinshaw Baylis, J. (1997). Sex, Symbols and Dreams. Seal Beach, CA: Sun, Man, Moon.

Spiritual Dream Interpretation

Coburn, Chuck. (1999). Reality Is Just an Illusion. Saint Paul, MN: Liewellyn Publications.

Hoffman, Edward. (1981). The Way of Slendor: Jewish Mysticism and Modern Psychology. Boulder, CO: Shambhala Publications.

Monford, H. (1994). Studies in Jewish Dream Interpretation. Lanham, MD: Rowman & Littlefield/Jason Aronson.

Pike, D. K. (1996). Life as a Waking Dream. New York, NY: Berkley Publishing Group.

Reed, H., & English, B. (2000). The Intuitive Heart: How to Trust Your Intuition for Guidance and Healing. Virginia Beach, VA: Association for Research and Enlightenment.

Transition

Sheehy, G. (1974). Passages. Predictable Crisis of Adult Life. New York, NY: Bantam Books.

Siegal, A. B. (1996). Dreams That Can Change Your Life. New York, NY: Berkley Publishing Group.

Spencer, S. A., & Adams, J. D. (1990). Life Changes: Growing Through Personal Transitions. San Luis Obispo, CA: Impact Publishers.